THE CAREER IDEAS FOR KIDS SERIES

Second Edition

DIANE LINDSEY REEVES

with
LINDSEY CLASEN

Illustrations by
NANCY BOND

Checkmark Books®
An imprint of Infobase Publishing

CAREER IDEAS FOR KIDS WHO LIKE ART, Second Edition

Copyright © 2007, 1998 by Diane Lindsey Reeves

Checkmark Books
An imprint of Infobase Publishing
132 West 31st Street
New York NY 10001

ISBN-10: 0-8160-6542-X
ISBN-13: 978-0-8160-6542-4

Library of Congress Cataloging-in-Publication Data
Reeves, Diane Lindsey, 1959–
    Career ideas for kids who like art / Diane Lindsey Reeves ; with Lindsey
Clasen ; illustrations by Nancy Bond. — 2nd ed.
      p. cm. — (The career ideas for kids series)
    Includes index.
    ISBN 0-8160-6541-1 (hc : alk. paper) — ISBN 0-8160-6542-X (pb : alk. paper)
1. Arts—Vocational guidance—United States—Juvenile literature. I. Clasen,
Lindsey. II. Bond, Nancy. III. Reeves, Diane Lindsey, 1959– Art. IV. Title.
V. Series: Reeves, Diane Lindsey, 1959– Career ideas for kids who like.
    NX503.R44 2007
    700.23'73—dc22   2006017879

Checkmark Books are available at special discounts when purchased in bulk quantities for businesses, associations, institutions, or sales promotions. Please call our Special Sales Department in New York at (212) 967-8800 or (800) 322-8755.

You can find Facts On File on the World Wide Web at http://www.factsonfile.com

Original text and cover design by Smart Graphics
Illustrations by Nancy Bond

Printed in the United States of America

MP Hermitage 10 9 8 7 6 5 4 3 2 1

This book is printed on acid-free paper.

CONTENTS

ACKNOWLEDGMENTS

A million thanks to the people who took the time to share their career stories and provide photos for this book:

June Beckstead
Jim Caron
Ariella Chezar
Laurent Dufourg
Mary Engelbreit
Michael Graves
Anthony Grieder
Kaki Hockersmith
Judith Jamison
Barbara Luck
Rusty Mills
Gary Pettit
Stephen Shames
Steven Shipley
Richard Steckel

Finally, much appreciation and admiration is due to all the behind-the-scenes people at Ferguson who have done so much to make this series all that it is. With extra thanks to James Chambers and Sarah Fogarty.

MAKE A CHOICE!

Choices.

You make them every day. What do I want for breakfast? Which shirt can I pull out of the dirty-clothes hamper to wear to school today? Should I finish my homework or play video games?

Some choices don't make much difference in the overall scheme of things. Face it; who really cares whether you wear the blue shirt or the red one?

Other choices are a major big deal. Figuring out what you want to be when you grow up is one of those all-important choices.

But, you say, you're just a kid. How are you supposed to know what you want to do with your life?

You're right: 10, 11, 12, and even 13 are a bit young to know exactly what and where and how you're going to do whatever it is you're going to do as an adult. But it's the perfect time to start making some important discoveries about who you are, what you like to do, and what you do best. It's a great time to start exploring the options and experimenting with different ideas. In fact, there's never a better time to mess around with different career ideas without messing up your life.

When it comes to picking a career, you've basically got two choices.

CHOICE A

You can be like lots of other people and just go with the flow. Float through school doing only what you absolutely have to in order to graduate, take any job you can find, collect a paycheck, and meander your way to retirement without making much of a splash in life.

Although many people take this route and do just fine, others end up settling for second best. They miss out on a meaningful education, satisfying work, and the rewards of a focused and well-planned career. That's why this path is not an especially good idea for someone who actually wants to have a life.

CHOICE B

Other people get a little more involved in choosing a career. They figure out what they want to accomplish in their lives—whether it's making a difference, making lots of money, or simply enjoying what they do. Then they find out what it takes to reach that goal, and they set about doing it with gusto. It's kind of like these people do things on purpose instead of letting life happen by accident.

Choosing A is like going to an ice cream parlor where there are all kinds of awesome flavors and ordering a single scoop of plain vanilla. Going with Choice B is more like visiting that same ice cream parlor and ordering a super duper brownie sundae drizzled with hot fudge, smothered in whip cream, and topped with a big red cherry.

Do you see the difference?

Reading this book is a great idea for kids who want to go after life in a big way. It provides a first step toward learning about careers that match your skills, values, and dreams. It will help you make the most out of your time in school and maybe even inspire you to—as the U.S. Army so proudly says—"be all that you can be."

Ready for the challenge of Choice B? If so, read the next section for instructions on how to get started.

HOW TO USE THIS BOOK

This book isn't just about interesting careers that other people have. It's also a book about interesting careers that you can have.

Of course, it won't do you a bit of good to just read this book. To get the whole shebang, you're going to have to jump in with both feet, roll up your sleeves, put on your thinking cap—whatever it takes—to help you do these three things:

🔆 Discover what you do best and enjoy the most. (This is the secret ingredient for finding work that's perfect for you.)

- ☿ Explore ways to match your interests and abilities with career ideas.
- ☿ Experiment with lots of different ideas until you find the ideal career. (It's like trying on all kinds of hats to see which ones fit!)

Use this book as a road map to some exciting career destinations. Here's what to expect in the chapters that follow.

GET IN GEAR!

First stop: discover. These activities will help you uncover important clues about the special traits and abilities that make you *you*. When you are finished you will have developed a personal Skill Set that will help guide you to career ideas in the next chapter.

TAKE A TRIP!

Next stop: explore. Cruise down the career idea highway and find out about a variety of career ideas that are especially appropriate for people who like art. Use the Skill Set chart at the beginning of each career profile to match your own interests with those required for success on the job.

Once you've identified a career that interests you, kick your exploration into high gear by checking out some of the Web sites, library resources, and professional organizations listed at the end of each career profile. For an extra challenge, follow the instructions for the Try It Out activity.

MAKE AN ARTISTIC DETOUR!

Here's your chance to explore up-and-coming opportunities in computer graphics and animation as well as the tried-and-true fields of fine arts, teaching, and basic design.

Just when you thought you'd seen it all, here come dozens of interesting art ideas to add to the career mix. Charge up

your career search by learning all you can about some of these opportunities.

DON'T STOP NOW!

Third stop: experiment. The library, the telephone, a computer, and a mentor—four keys to a successful career planning adventure. Use them well, and before long you'll be on the trail of some hot career ideas of your own.

WHAT'S NEXT?

Make a plan! Chart your course (or at least the next stop) with these career planning road maps. Whether you're moving full steam ahead with a great idea or get slowed down at a yellow light of indecision, these road maps will keep you moving forward toward a great future.

Use a pencil—you're bound to make a detour or two along the way. But, hey, you've got to start somewhere.

HOORAY! YOU DID IT!

Some final rules of the road before sending you off to new adventures.

SOME FUTURE DESTINATIONS

This section lists a few career planning tools you'll want to know about.

You've got a lot of ground to cover in this phase of your career planning journey. Start your engines and get ready for an exciting adventure!

Career planning is a lifelong journey. There's usually more than one way to get where you're going, and there are often some interesting detours along the way. But you have to start somewhere. So rev up and find out all you can about one-of-a-kind, specially designed you. That's the first stop on what can be the most exciting trip of your life!

To get started, complete the five exercises described throughout the following pages.

DISCOVER #1: WATCH FOR SIGNS ALONG THE WAY

Road signs help drivers figure out how to get where they want to go. They provide clues about direction, road conditions, and safety. Your career road signs will provide clues about who you are, what you like, and what you do best. These clues can help you decide where to look for the career ideas that are best for you.

Complete the following statements to make them true for you. There are no right or wrong reasons. Jot down the response that describes you best. Your answers will provide important clues about career paths you should explore.

Please Note: If this book does not belong to you, write your responses on a separate sheet of paper.

On my last report card, I got the best grade in _____ .

On my last report card, I got the worst grade in _____ .

I am happiest when _____ .

Something I can do for hours without getting bored is _____ .

Something that bores me out of my mind is

_____ .

My favorite class is _____ .

My least favorite class is _____ .

The one thing I'd like to accomplish is

_____ .

My favorite thing to do after school is

_____ .

My least favorite thing to do after school
is _____ .

Something I'm really good at is _____ .

Something really tough for me to do
is _____ .

My favorite adult person is _____
because _____ .

When I grow up _____ .

The kinds of books I like to read are
about _____ .

The kinds of videos I like to watch are
about _____ .

DISCOVER #2: RULES OF THE ROAD

Pretty much any job you can think of involves six common ingredients. Whether the work requires saving the world or selling bananas, all work revolves around a central **purpose** or reason for existing. All work is conducted somewhere, in some **place**, whether it's on the 28th floor of a city sky-scraper or on a cruise ship in the middle of an ocean. All work requires a certain **time** commitment and is performed using various types of **tools**. **People** also play an important part in most jobs—whether the job involves interacting with lots or very few of them. And, especially from where you are sitting as a kid still in school, all work involves some type of **preparation** to learn how to do the job.

Another word for these six common ingredients is "values." Each one represents important aspects of work that people value in different ways. The following activity will give you a chance to think about what matters most to you in each of these areas. That way you'll get a better idea of things to look for as you explore different careers.

Here's how the process works:

First, read the statements listed for each value on the following pages. Decide which, if any, represent your idea of an ideal job.

Next, take a look at the grid on page 16. For every value statement with which you agreed, draw its symbol in the appropriate space on your grid. (If this book doesn't belong to you, use a blank sheet of paper to draw your own grid with six big spaces.) Or, if you want to get really fancy, cut pictures out of magazines and glue them into the appropriate space. If you do not see a symbol that represents your best answer, make up a new one and sketch it in the appropriate box.

When you are finished, you'll have a very useful picture of the kinds of values that matter most to you in your future job.

PURPOSE

Which of the following statements describes what you most hope to accomplish in your future work? Pick as many as are true for you and feel free to add others.

♥	❏	I want to help other people.
	❏	I want to make lots of money.
★	❏	I want to do something I really believe in.
	❏	I want to make things.
	❏	I want to use my brain power in challenging ways.
	❏	I want to work with my own creative ideas.
	❏	I want to be very successful.
	❏	I want to find a good company and stick with it for the rest of my life.
	❏	I want to be famous.

Other purpose-related things that are especially important to me are

		PLACE
	When you think about your future work, what kind of place would you most like to do it in? Pick as many as are true for you and feel free to add others.

	❑	I want to work in a big city skyscraper.
	❑	I want to work in a shopping mall or retail store.
	❑	I want to work in the great outdoors.
	❑	I want to travel a lot for my work.
	❑	I want to work out of my own home.
	❑	I want to work for a govern-ment agency.
	❑	I want to work in a school or university.
	❑	I want to work in a factory or laboratory.

Other place-related things that are especially important to me are

TIME

When you think about your future work, what kind of schedule sounds most appealing to you? Pick as many as are true for you and feel free to add others.

	❏	I'd rather work regular business hours—nine to five, Monday through Friday.
	❏	I'd like to have lots of vacation time.
	❏	I'd prefer a flexible schedule so I can balance my work, family, and personal needs.
	❏	I'd like to work nights only so my days are free.
	❏	I'd like to work where the pace is fast and I stay busy all day.
	❏	I'd like to work where I would always know exactly what I'm supposed to do.
	❏	I'd like to work where I could plan my own day.
	❏	I'd like to work where there's lots of variety and no two days are alike.

Other time-related things that are especially important to me are

![person]	❑	I'd prefer to work mostly with people.
![computer]	❑	I'd prefer to work mostly with technology.
![screws]	❑	I'd prefer to work mostly with machines.
![bag]	❑	I'd prefer to work mostly with products people buy.
![airplane]	❑	I'd prefer to work mostly with planes, trains, automobiles, or other things that go.
![head]	❑	I'd prefer to work mostly with ideas.
![book]	❑	I'd prefer to work mostly with information.
![tree]	❑	I'd prefer to work mostly with nature.

TOOLS

What kinds of things would you most like to work with? Pick as many as are true for you and feel free to add others.

Other tool-related things that are especially important to me are

PEOPLE

What role do other people play in your future work? How many do you want to interact with on a daily basis? What age group would you most enjoy working with? Pick as many as are true for you and feel free to add others.

	❏	I'd like to work with lots of people all day long.
	❏	I'd prefer to work alone most of the time.
	❏	I'd like to work as part of a team.
	❏	I'd like to work with people I might choose as friends.
	❏	I'd like to work with babies, children, or teenagers.
	❏	I'd like to work mostly with elderly people.
	❏	I'd like to work mostly with people who are in trouble.
	❏	I'd like to work mostly with people who are ill.

Other people-related things that are especially important to me are

PREPARATION		
When you think about your future work, how much time and energy do you want to devote to preparing for it? Pick as many as are true for you and feel free to add others.		
	❑	I want to find a job that requires a college degree.
	❑	I want to find a job where I could learn what I need to know on the job.
	❑	I want to find a job that requires no additional training after I graduate from high school.
	❑	I want to find a job where the more education I get, the better my chances for a better job.
	❑	I want to run my own business and be my own boss.
Other preparation-related things that are especially important to me are		

Now that you've uncovered some word clues about the types of values that are most important to you, use the grid on the following page (or use a separate sheet of paper if this book does not belong to your) to "paint a picture" of your ideal future career. Use the icons as ideas for how to visualize each statement. Or, if you'd like to get really creative, get a large sheet of paper, some markers, magazines, and glue or tape and create a collage.

PURPOSE	PLACE	TIME
TOOLS	**PEOPLE**	**PREPARATION**

DISCOVER #3: DANGEROUS DETOURS

Half of figuring out what you do want to do is figuring out what you don't want to do. Get a jump start on this process by making a list of 10 careers you already know you absolutely don't want to do.

Warning: Failure to heed early warnings signs to avoid careers like this can result in long hours of boredom and frustration spent doing a job you just weren't meant to do.

(If this book does not belong to you, make your list on a separate sheet of paper.)

1. _____   _____

2. _____   _____

3. _____   _____

4. _____   _____

5. _____   _____

6. _____   _____

7. _____   _____

8. _____   _____

9. _____   _____

10. _____   _____

Red Flag Summary:
Look over your list, and in the second column above (or on a separate sheet of paper) see if you can summarize what it is about these jobs that makes you want to avoid them like a bad case of cooties.

DISCOVER #4: ULTIMATE CAREER DESTINATION

Imagine that your dream job is like a favorite tourist destination and you have to convince other people to pick it over every other career in the world. How would you describe it? What features make it especially appealing to you? What does a person have to do to have a career like it?

Take a blank sheet of paper and fold it into thirds. Fill each column on both sides with words and pictures that create a vivid image of what you'd most like your future career to be.

Special note: Just for now, instead of actually naming a specific career, describe what your ideal career would be like. In places where the name of the career would be used, leave a blank space like this _____. For instance: For people who want to become rich and famous, being a _____ is the way to go.

DISCOVER #5: GET SOME DIRECTION

It's easy to get lost when you don't have a good idea of where you want to go. This is especially true when you start thinking about what to do with the rest of your life. Unless you focus on where you want to go, you might get lost or even miss the exit. This discover exercise will help you connect your own interests and abilities with a whole world of career opportunities.

Mark the activities that you enjoy doing or would enjoy doing if you had the chance. Be picky. Don't mark ideas that you wish you would do. Mark only those that you would really do. For instance, if skydiving sounds appealing but you'd never do it because you are terrified of heights, don't mark it.

Please Note: If this book does not belong to you, write your responses on a separate sheet of paper.

- ❏ 1. Rescue a cat stuck in a tree
- ❏ 2. Paint a mural on the cafeteria wall
- ❏ 3. Run for student council
- ❏ 4. Send e-mail to a "pen pal" in another state
- ❏ 5. Find out all there is to know about the American Revolution
- ❏ 6. Survey your classmates to find out what they do after school
- ❏ 7. Try out for the school play
- ❏ 8. Dissect a frog and identify the different organs
- ❏ 9. Play baseball, soccer, football, or _____ (fill in your favorite sport)

❏ 10. Talk on the phone to just about anyone who will talk back

❏ 11. Try foods from all over the world—Thailand, Poland, Japan, etc.

❏ 12. Write poems about things that are happening in your life

❏ 13. Create a really scary haunted house to take your friends through on Halloween

❏ 14. Bake a cake and decorate it for your best friend's birthday

❏ 15. Sell enough advertisements for the school year-book to win a trip to Walt Disney World

❏ 16. Simulate an imaginary flight through space on your computer screen

❏ 17. Collect stamps, coins, baseball cards, or whatever and organize them into a fancy display

❏ 18. Build model airplanes, boats, doll houses, or anything from kits

❏ 19. Teach your friends a new dance routine

❏ 20. Watch the stars come out at night and see how many constellations you can find

❏ 21. Watch baseball, soccer, football, or _____ (fill in your favorite sport) on TV

❏ 22. Give a speech in front of the entire school

❏ 23. Plan the class field trip to Washington, D.C.

❏ 24. Read everything in sight, including the back of the cereal box

❏ 25. Figure out "who dunnit" in a mystery story

❏ 26. Make a poster announcing the school football game

❏ 27. Think up a new way to make the lunch line move faster and explain it to the cafeteria staff

❏ 28. Put together a multimedia show for a school assembly using music and lots of pictures and graphics

❏ 29. Visit historic landmarks like the Statue of Liberty and Civil War battlegrounds

❏ 30. Invest your allowance in the stock market and keep track of how it does

❏ 31. Go to the ballet or opera every time you get the chance

❏ 32. Do experiments with a chemistry set

❏ 33. Keep score at your sister's Little League game

34. Use lots of funny voices when reading stories to children

35. Ride on airplanes, trains, boats—anything that moves

36. Interview the new exchange student for an article in the school newspaper

37. Build your own treehouse

38. Visit an art museum and pickout your favorite painting

39. Play Monopoly in an all-night championship challenge

40. Make a chart on the computer to show how much soda students buy from the school vending machines each week

41. Find out all you can about your family ancestors and make a family tree

42. Keep track of how much your team earns to buy new uniforms

43. Play an instrument in the school band or orchestra

44. Take things apart and put them back together again

45. Write stories about sports for the school newspaper

46. Listen to other people talk about their problems

❑ 47. Imagine yourself in exotic places
❑ 48. Hang around bookstores and libraries
❑ 49. Play harmless practical jokes on April Fools' Day
❑ 50. Take photographs at the school talent show
❑ 51. Make money by setting up your own business—
paper route, lemonade stand, etc.
❑ 52. Create an imaginary city using a computer
❑ 53. Look for Native American artifacts and arrowheads
❑ 54. Do 3-D puzzles
❑ 55. Keep track of the top 10 songs of the week
❑ 56. Read about famous inventors and their inventions
❑ 57. Make play-by-play announcements at the school
football game
❑ 58. Answer the phones during a telethon to raise
money for orphans
❑ 59. Be an exchange student in another country
❑ 60. Write down all your secret thoughts and favorite
sayings in a journal
❑ 61. Jump out of an airplane (with a parachute, of course)
❑ 62. Use a video camera to make your own movies

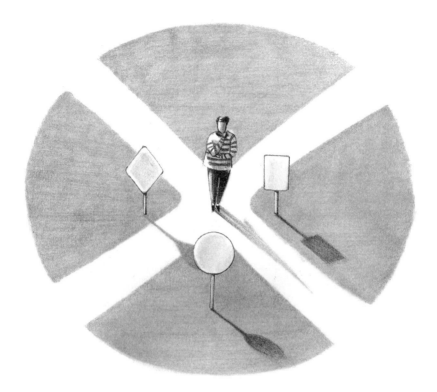

❏ 63. Get your friends together to help clean up your town after a hurricane or other natural disaster

❏ 64. Spend your summer at a computer camp learning lots of new computer programs

❏ 65. Help your little brother or sister make ink out of blueberry juice

❏ 66. Build bridges, skyscrapers, and other structures out of LEGOs

❏ 67. Plan a concert in the park for little kids

❏ 68. Collect different kinds of rocks

❏ 69. Help plan a sports tournament

❏ 70. Be DJ for the school dance

❏ 71. Learn how to fly a plane or sail a boat

❏ 72. Write funny captions for pictures in the school yearbook

❏ 73. Scuba dive to search for buried treasure

❏ 74. Sketch pictures of your friends

❏ 75. Pick out neat stuff to sell at the school store
❏ 76. Answer your classmates' questions about how to use the computer
❏ 77. Make a timeline showing important things that happened during the year
❏ 78. Draw a map showing how to get to your house from school
❏ 79. Make up new words to your favorite songs
❏ 80. Take a hike and name the different kinds of trees, birds, or flowers
❏ 81. Referee intramural basketball games
❏ 82. Join the school debate team
❏ 83. Make a poster with postcards from all the places you went on your summer vacation
❏ 84. Write down stories that your grandparents tell you about when they were young

CALCULATE THE CLUES

Now is your chance to add it all up. Each of the 12 boxes on these pages contains an interest area that is common to both your world and the world of work. Follow these directions to discover your personal Skill Set:

1. Find all of the numbers that you checked on pages 18–23 in the

boxes below and mark them with an X. Work your
way all the way through number 84.

2. Go back and count the Xs marked for each interest area. Write that number in the space that says
"Total."

3. Find the interest area with the highest total and put
a number one in the "Rank" blank of that box. Repeat
this process for the next two highest scoring areas.
Rank the second highest as number two and the third
highest as number three.

4. If you have more than three strong areas, choose the
three that are most important and interesting to you.

**Remember: If this book does not belong to you, write your
responses on a separate sheet of paper.**

ADVENTURE

❏ 1
❏ 13
❏ 25
❏ 37
❏ 49
❏ 61
❏ 73
Total: _____
Rank: _____

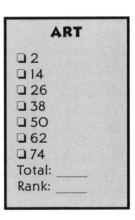

ART

❏ 2
❏ 14
❏ 26
❏ 38
❏ 50
❏ 62
❏ 74
Total: _____
Rank: _____

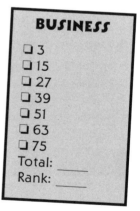

BUSINESS

❏ 3
❏ 15
❏ 27
❏ 39
❏ 51
❏ 63
❏ 75
Total: _____
Rank: _____

COMPUTERS

- ❏ 4
- ❏ 16
- ❏ 28
- ❏ 40
- ❏ 52
- ❏ 64
- ❏ 76

Total: _____

Rank: _____

HISTORY

- ❏ 5
- ❏ 17
- ❏ 29
- ❏ 41
- ❏ 53
- ❏ 65
- ❏ 77

Total: _____

Rank: _____

MATH

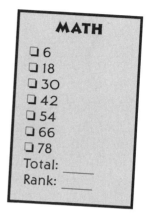

- ❏ 6
- ❏ 18
- ❏ 30
- ❏ 42
- ❏ 54
- ❏ 66
- ❏ 78

Total: _____

Rank: _____

MUSIC/DANCE

- ❏ 7
- ❏ 19
- ❏ 31
- ❏ 43
- ❏ 55
- ❏ 67
- ❏ 79

Total: _____

Rank: _____

SCIENCE

- ❏ 8
- ❏ 20
- ❏ 32
- ❏ 44
- ❏ 56
- ❏ 68
- ❏ 80

Total: _____

Rank: _____

SPORTS

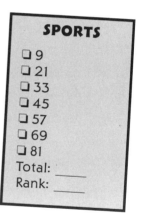

- ❏ 9
- ❏ 21
- ❏ 33
- ❏ 45
- ❏ 57
- ❏ 69
- ❏ 81

Total: _____

Rank: _____

TALKING

- ❏ 10
- ❏ 22
- ❏ 34
- ❏ 46
- ❏ 58
- ❏ 70
- ❏ 82

Total: _____

Rank: _____

TRAVEL

- ❏ 11
- ❏ 23
- ❏ 35
- ❏ 47
- ❏ 59
- ❏ 71
- ❏ 83

Total: _____

Rank: _____

WRITING

- ❏ 12
- ❏ 24
- ❏ 36
- ❏ 48
- ❏ 60
- ❏ 72
- ❏ 84

Total: _____

Rank: _____

What are your top three interest areas? List them here (or on a separate piece of paper).

1. _____

2. _____

3. _____

This is your personal Skill Set and provides important clues about the kinds of work you're most likely to enjoy. Remember it and look for career ideas with a skill set that matches yours most closely. You'll find a Skill Set box at the beginning of each career profile in the following section.

TAKE A TRIP!

Cruise down the
career idea highway
and enjoy in-depth pro-
files of some of the interesting options in this field. Keep in
mind all that you've discovered about yourself so far. Find the
careers that match your own Skill Set first. Then keep thinking
about the other ideas—exploration is the name of this game.

The following profiles introduce a variety of artistic careers.
You may be surprised to learn that there are so many options
that rely heavily on artistic ability and creative thinking.

Perhaps more than any other professional field, the artistic field relies on show-and-tell—with an emphasis on show.
Many of these professions are visually oriented. As you read
these profiles, see if you can paint a mental picture of what
each career would involve.

Also, as you read about each career, imagine yourself doing the job, and ask yourself the following questions:

☀ Would I like it?
☀ Would I be good at it?
☀ Is it the stuff my career dreams are made of?

If so, make a quick exit to explore what it involves, try it out, check it out, and get acquainted! Look out for the symbols below.

Buckle up and enjoy the trip!

 **TRY IT OUT**

 **CHECK IT OUT**

 **ON THE WEB**

 **AT THE LIBRARY**

 **WITH THE EXPERTS**

A NOTE ON WEB SITES

Internet sites tend to move around the Web a bit. If you have trouble finding a particular site, use an Internet browser to find a specific Web site or type of information.

Actor

SKILL SET

✔ ADVENTURE

✔ ART

✔ TALKING

SHORTCUTS

GO take as many speech, voice, movement, and drama classes as you can.

READ biographies of some of your favorite stars.

TRY auditioning for school and community theater performances.

WHAT IS AN ACTOR?

Ready. Set. Action!

With those three words, actors assume new identities, go back or forward in time, and temporarily lose themselves in a fictional life in order to entertain, educate, or enlighten others. Good actors are so convincing that it's nearly impossible to separate the "real" people from the roles they've assumed.

Along with the ability to act convincingly, a great memory and thick skin are two other assets that actors must possess in great abundance. Actors must memorize entire scenes and recall countless genuine gestures and expressions. Above all, actors must be able to bounce back from the inevitable (and

29

often frequent) rejection that's part of this competitive profession. It takes a healthy dose of self-confidence and a deep commitment to acting to weather the ups and downs that are a normal part of life for all actors.

Acting is one of those "glamour" careers; it's so attractive that there are more starstruck actors than there are starring roles. That's why aspiring actors are often advised to "keep their day jobs." Maybe even more than with other careers, those who aspire to become actors must do so with their eyes open. And they need a good backup plan for earning a living while waiting for their "lucky break."

Keep in mind that Hollywood and Broadway aren't the only places to make a living as an actor. Other ways to satisfy the acting "itch" while keeping a roof over your head include performing in the following settings:

- community theater
- dinner theater clubs
- commercials
- educational videos
- theme-park productions

You might even want to consider teaching drama in a high school or coaching a children's theater program.

While it's true that only a few actors become superstars, it might just as well be you. So, hold tight to your dreams, make decisions carefully, and find creative ways to combine your interest in acting with making a living. Just remember, if you've got the acting bug—the show must go on!

 TRY IT OUT

MIRROR, MIRROR ON THE WALL

Act out the following scenes (emotions, appropriate expressions, and all):

- getting caught in a lie
- sitting at the bedside of a friend dying

☼ reacting to winning the lottery jackpot
☼ proposing marriage to a reluctant partner
☼ greeting a long-lost sibling

At first, you may want to find a place where you can prac-tice by yourself. Don't be trite or predictable in your responses. Try to be genuine, natural, and spontaneous.

Ask a friend or a parent to use digital cameras, camera phones, or disposal cameras to takes pictures of you in each pose. Make a poster showcasing the best results.

ACTING SCHOOL FOR ONE

Every year since 1927 the prestigious Academy of Motion Pictures Arts and Sciences awards Oscars to honor what they consider the best performances and movies. As an aspiring actor, you can learn a lot by watching these movies and studying the way actors perform. You can find copies of many Oscar award-winning movies at your local video store or, in some cases, at your public library.

Make it official by keeping an Oscar log to record your observations about each film. Try to watch movies made dur-ing different decades and compare the differences between older films and more recent ones. For complete lists of these films, go online to the official Academy Web site at http:// www.oscars.org or check out the greatest films lists at http:// www.filmsite.org.

HOLLYWOOD, HERE I COME!

Summer drama camps for young people are located through-out the United States and in other parts of the world. You may also find a variety of after-school programs to choose from during the rest of the year. Any of these programs provides opportunities to learn the ropes in small productions, and they can be lots of fun. To find out about programs in your area, contact recreation centers, performing arts centers, and school drama teachers.

Two exceptionally good national programs that may be worth your consideration include

Missoula Children's Theatre (MCT Inc.)
200 North Adams Street
Missoula, MT 59802-4718
http://www.mctinc.org

Children's Theatre Company
2400 Third Avenue South
Minneapolis, MN 55404-3506
http://www.childrenstheatre.org

Once you have a little experience under your belt, you might want to consider getting involved in summer stock theater (summer camp programs for actors in which participants spend their time preparing for a special production). Programs of this type tend to be a bit more professional and are often an important early step in a budding career. To find out about nearby programs, look online at the Summer Theater Resource Center at http://www.summertheater.com or the casting announcements listed at http://www.backstage.com/backstage/casting/index.jsp.

HELP WANTED
Scour the "audition" section in the classified advertisements of your local newspaper (the larger and more "artsy" the town, the more listings you'll find). Listings might include productions at colleges, community theaters, dinner theaters, and other centers. Look for roles that fit your age, gender, and experience level.

Find out all you can about the various roles and the audition requirements. Plan and practice an audition performance. Be prepared with an acting résumé and photographs of yourself. Take a chance and go for it!

If you aren't quite ready for the real thing yet, find out if the local library subscribes to trade magazines like *Billboard*, *Daily Variety*, or *Variety*. If so, look for a dream role and make a plan for getting it, although it will be a fictional plan at this point.

Think about the following questions: What image would you want to project? What would you wear? What type of scene would you prepare for the audition? Would you have to sing? Dance?

If the library doesn't have copies of these magazines, look for current copies of them at a larger bookstore or visit their Web sites at:

Billboard
Billboard Publications
http://www.billboard.com

Variety
http//:www.variety.com

CHECK IT OUT

ON THE WEB

ONLINE DRAMA

All the Web is a stage! Find a variety of resources for young actors at these Web sites:

- Explore one of Shakespeare's most famous plays at http://www.clicknotes.com/romeo/welcome.html.
- Find out how Hollywood films are made at http://www.learner.org/exhibits/cinema.
- Go behind the scenes of a theater production at http://www.artsalive.ca/en/eth/design/index.html.
- Read about some of your favorite kid actors at http://www.kidactors.com.
- Look for summer drama camps near you at http://www.petersons.com/summerop; http://www.campchannel.com; and http://www.summercamps.com.

AT THE LIBRARY

BEHIND THE SCENES

It's not just *who* you know; it's also *what* you know that can make things happen for you as an actor. Learn all you can about acting and the behind-the-scenes aspects of the profession.

For an introduction to acting, try:

Friedman, Lisa. *Break a Leg! The Kid's Guide to Acting and Stagecraft.* New York: Workman, 2002.

To hone your skills as an actor, try some of the activities featured in:

Milstein, Janet. *The Ultimate Monologue Book for Middle School Actors: 111 One-Minute Monologues.* Lyme, N.H.: Smith and Kraus Books for Kids, 2005.

Slaight, Craig. *Great Monologues for Young Actors.* Lyme, N.H.: Smith and Kraus Books for Kids, 2005.

———. *Great Scenes for Young Actors.* Lyme, N.H.: Smith and Kraus Books for Kids, 2005.

Winters, Lisa Bany. *Funny Bones: Comedy Games and Activities for Kids.* Chicago: Chicago Review Press, 2002.

———. *On Stage: Theater Games and Activities for Kids.* Chicago: Chicago Review Press, 1997.

———. *Show Time: Music, Dance and Drama Activities for Kids.* Chicago: Chicago Review Press, 2000.

And, finally, top off your act with some science with:

Cobb, Vicki. *On Stage: Where's the Science Here.* Minneapolis: Millbrook Press, 2005.

🗣 WITH THE EXPERTS

Actor's Equity Association
165 West 46th Street
New York, NY 10036-2501
http://www.actorsequity.org

American Alliance for Theater and Education
7475 Wisconsin Avenue, Suite 300A
Bethesda, MD 20814-3412
http://www.aate.com

American Association of Community Theater
8402 Briarwood Circle
Lago Vista, TX 78645-4118
http://www.aact.org

Screen Actors Guild
5757 Wilshire Boulevard
Los Angeles, CA 90036-4118
http://www.sag.org

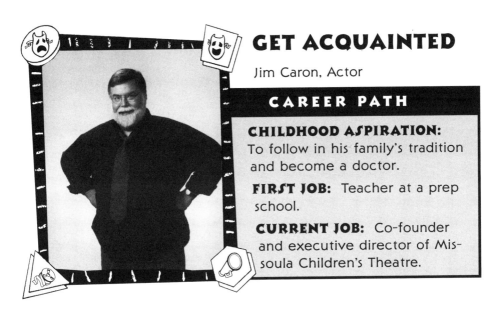

GET ACQUAINTED

Jim Caron, Actor

CAREER PATH

CHILDHOOD ASPIRATION:
To follow in his family's tradition and become a doctor.

FIRST JOB: Teacher at a prep school.

CURRENT JOB: Co-founder and executive director of Missoula Children's Theatre.

A funny thing happened to Jim Caron when he was driving cross country to his friend's wedding. First, his VW hippie van broke down in Montana. That was not funny. But, while he was waiting for it to get fixed he happened to notice a poster announcing auditions for a community production of the play

Man of La Mancha. With nothing better to do while waiting for his car to be repaired, Caron auditioned for the role of Sancho and—to his pleasant surprise—got the part.

Which meant that after attending the wedding in Oregon he returned to Montana for rehearsals. Little did he know at the time that the production would change his life forever.

For one thing, he absolutely fell in love with Montana. For another, he made what has become a lifelong best friend with the man who played the role of Don Quixote, named Don Collins. Together, the men decided to start a children's theater and named it the Missoula Children's Theatre.

SCRIPTED FOR SUCCESS

That was in 1970. Today the Missoula Children's Theatre works with over 65,000 children a year in all 50 United States and in 27 foreign countries. To say that the program exceeded Caron's wildest dreams is an understatement. Working from a state-of-the-art theater complex in Missoula, Caron and his home staff of 70 or so employees train some of the most promising young drama graduates to travel around the world directing children's plays. He says that Missoula was actually the first performance experience of many of these new "directors" and that some have been part of the program for years—starting as young performers, attending the summer camp programs in Missoula, working as camp counselors, and finally graduating from college to become directors.

Teams of two or three directors are invited into a community in the United States or abroad to conduct a week-long program. On the first day, children audition for roles in an original production with an average of 50 children winning roles. The next few days involve well-organized rehearsals capped off by a Saturday performance complete with professional-quality props and costumes. The amazing part is that all this is accomplished in just a week's time!

SMART MOVES

Given his long and very successful career, Caron says that there are two smart things he's done. First, he's surrounded himself with other smart, good people. Even in his hippie days as a young man, he avoided the drugs and other negative behaviors that were prevalent in that culture. Instead, he chose to live his life with character and build his career by upholding strong ethics and always trying to do the right thing.

The second key to his success is that whenever a window of opportunity opened for him he was never afraid to leap through. He admits that there were times when he had to "crawl back out" later, but a willingness to try new things and follow his dreams has worked out well for him.

ACTING 101

The way Caron sees it, "acting recreates life." He says the best actors are the ones who actually have a life. He cautions kids against getting so caught up in theater life (which can be all-consuming) that they miss out on opportunities to round out their experiences through sports, travel, and other social activities. His best advice to aspiring actors is to "become an interesting person."

To find out more about the Missoula Children's Theatre, go online to http://www.mctinc.org.

Animator

SHORTCUTS

SKILL SET

✔ ART

✔ ADVENTURE

✔ WRITING

GO to animated movies and study TV cartoons.

READ comic books, the paper's funnies, and political cartoons.

TRY drawing cartoon characters and making up jokes.

WHAT IS AN ANIMATOR?

Animation Magazine's Web site says it best: "Animation has quickly become one of the most accessible artforms in the world today. From Mickey Mouse's Steamboat Willie to the most technologically advanced computer animation such as that used in *Toy Story*, the field has become a limitless icon of imagination for children and adults from all walks of life."

Whew! So you think using your artistic talents to make people laugh would be a fun way to make a living? Take this test to see if you could make it as a professional animator.

Pretend you've been hired by a studio to draw pictures for an animated cartoon show. As you're walking to your new workstation, the producer explains that in order to stay on schedule, you'll need to draw cartoons for 10 to 20 feet of film each week. There are 16 drawings per foot of film. What happens when you multiply that? You'll need to produce 160 to 320 drawings each week. If that doesn't scare you off, keep reading.

Animation is a challenging, highly creative artistic endeavor. Quality and quantity count in this profession. Consider these tidbits about Disney's animated film *Beauty and the Beast*: the film contained 1,295 painted backgrounds, included 120,000 drawings, and involved 370 people in its production (43 were animators).

Of course, computers take much of the mindless repetition out of the task, but even the most powerful technology cannot replace creative imagination. Animators use it by the gallon!

Artistic talent is crucial, but it's just one of the required skills. Animators need to know as much about current events and human nature as they do about art and drawing. They need to understand how people think and why they do the things they do. They need to see the humor in everyday situations. Some cartoonists look at the dark humor or satire in important social issues.

Although there are no official education requirements for animators, it is obvious that the more you know, the more places you can go. Some animators choose trade school training in graphic design, while others pursue training in special art schools. Still others may opt for a liberal arts education at a four-year college. Experience, lots of practice, and a great portfolio are the keys to getting your foot in the door for a good job. The portfolio is especially important because it showcases your talent. A good one can be the ticket to your dream job.

Animators don't just work on movies. Newspapers, magazines, advertising firms, greeting card companies, and book publishers are other professional outlets for animators. New developments in multimedia, CD-ROM, computer games, and educational software are providing a wave of exciting opportunities for those with both artistic and computer skills.

Opportunity is out there. Work hard and prove that you've got the talent to make it on a professional level. Who knows? Maybe you'll become the next Walt Disney.

 **TRY IT OUT**

SKETCHES TO GO

It goes without saying that if you want to be an animator, you need to learn how to draw cartoons. In fact, here is the first rule for any potential artist: Don't leave home without your sketchbook. Sketch scenes at school, objects lying around the house, images from nature, and even other people. Create your own illustrations for a favorite book. Sketch during your favorite television shows. You get the picture—draw anything and everything in sight.

If you aren't driving your family crazy with all your artwork, you aren't drawing enough!

ARTISTIC EXERCISES

You might be surprised at other techniques that some of the best animators use to hone their craft. Following are several ideas that will help you perfect your skills.

Take a dance class. Sure, you can enjoy the exercise and all the great music, but as a potential animator you need an ulterior motive as well. Watch how the human body moves. Notice the angles and alignment. Even though your cartoon characters are likely to be caricatures of humans, they still need realistic human qualities that make them come alive.

Go to the zoo. Study the various animals and watch their reactions as they interact with other animals and people. What happens to a lion's mane when it roars? What about its tail and hind quarters? Be alert and teach yourself to notice the tiniest movements and reactions.

Be a people watcher. Airports are a people watcher's paradise. You'll catch an amazing array of emotions and reactions: the frantic traveler scurrying to catch his plane; the grandparents seeing their new grandchild for the first time; the tearful family saying good-bye to a son or daughter in military uniform. Make up stories to go along with each situation that you observe.

Get some culture. A great place to study human movement is at the ballet. Ask if you can sit in the balcony and sketch the dancers during their rehearsals.

Take a drama class. Animators are actors with a pencil. Learning how to act will teach you to understand how different characters would respond to different situations. It takes you out of yourself and into the lives and minds of strangers.

Tell a story. Volunteer to read stories to children at your local day care center or library. Animators tell stories with their drawings. Reading out loud gives you a feel for the structure and pacing of a good story. Be sure to keep a journal to record your discoveries and sketch your observations.

TRICKS OF THE TRADE

As with any career, one of the best sources of information about animation comes from people who are already succeeding in the field. You have a special edge in animation because you can simply tune in to some of your favorite channels on television. Check out the following kid-friendly Web sites and pick at least one show from each network to explore:

- ‍ Cartoon Network, at http://www.cartoonnetwork.com
- ‍ Disney Channel, at http://www.disney.com
- ‍ Nickelodeon, at http://www.nick.com
- ‍ Warner Brothers, at http://looneytunes.warnerbros.com

Make a chart with space to record what you learn about each of the four shows you pick. Make notes about the main characters, special techniques, and fun touches that you notice. Make a sketch of one of your favorite characters for each show.

CHECK IT OUT

ON THE WEB

ONLINE ANIMATION

Take your animation exploration into cyberspace by visiting some of these interesting Web sites:

- Find cartoon drawing lessons and kooky games at http://www.cooltoons.com.
- Visit the Web site of Pixar Animation Studio for information about some of your favorite animated movies at http://www.pixar.com.
- How does TV animation work? Find out for yourself at http://entertainment.howstuffworks.com/tv-animation. htm.
- Learn how to draw cartoons at http://www.kidsdraw. com.
- Animation Artist features all the latest information, news, and interviews on animation projects and animation artists at http://www.animationartist.com.

BEHIND THE SCENES

Go behind the scenes with some famous animators at the following Web sites:

- Learn about Paul Fierlinger and his dogs at http://www.pbs.org/itvs/animateddogs.
- Encounter Pulitzer Prize–winning cartoonist Rube Goldberg at http://www.rubegoldberg.com.
- Meet the creator of Wile E. Coyote at http://www.chuckjones.com.
- Discover the legacy of the late Charles Schultz at http://www.snoopy.com.
- Find inspiration of the story of Walt Disney at http://www.waltdisney.com.

And read about what it's really like to work in animation:

Riedl, Sue. _Career Diary of an Animation Producer: Thirty Days Behind the Scenes With a Professional._ Washington, DC: Garth Gardner, 2003.

AT THE LIBRARY

ADVENTURES IN ANIMATING

See yourself in the funny papers by trying some of the ideas described in books such as:

Barnhart, Duane. _Cartooning Basics: Creating the Characters and More._ White Bear Lake, Minn.: Cartoon Connections Press, 2004.

Blitz, Bruce. _Big Book of Cartooning._ Philadelphia: Running Press, 2001.

Hart, Christopher. _Cartooning for the Beginner._ New York: Watson Guptill, 2000.

Lightfoot, Marge. _Cartooning for Kids._ Toronto, Ontario: Maple Tree Press, 2004.

Roche, Art. _Art for Kids: Cartooning._ Asheville, N.C.: Lark, 2005.

WITH THE EXPERTS

For Information about Cartoonists, contact the following organization:

American Institute of Graphic Arts
164 Fifth Avenue
New York, NY 10010-5901
http://www.aiga.org

Animation Guild
4729 Lankershim Boulevard
North Hollywood, CA 91602-1803
http://www.mpsc839.org

Animation World Network
6525 Sunset Boulevard, Suite 10
Hollywood, CA 90028-7212
http://awn.com

National Cartoonists Society
1133 West Morse Boulevard, Suite 201
Winter Park, FL 32789-3727
http://www.reuben.org

Society of Children's Book Writers and Illustrators
8271 Beverly Boulevard
Los Angeles, CA 90048-4515
http://www.scbwi.org

GET ACQUAINTED

Rusty Mills, Animator and
Television Producer

CAREER PATH

CHILDHOOD ASPIRATION: To be an artist.

FIRST JOB: Making drawings of toys for a major toy company.

CURRENT JOB: Timing Director at Walt Disney Television Animation.

A childhood trip to the brand-new Walt Disney World decided Rusty Mills's future. He was so intrigued by the atmosphere that he wrote to the company as soon as he got home to find out how they did all that neat animation stuff. Much to his pleasure, someone wrote back and told him all about what it was like to be an animator.

Mills was also told that he would need a special camera to film his own cartoons. His father, who is also an artist, made a deal with Mills. If Mills painted the house, his dad would buy him the camera. The house got painted, Mills got his camera, and an exciting career was born.

A LITTLE LESSON LEARNED ALONG THE WAY

Never, ever send your own version of a popular cartoon character to its creator. Rusty learned this the hard way when he sent drawings of a famous duck to its famous creator. The duck's creator was not amused. He kindly suggested that Mills develop his own ideas.

The obvious lesson is that the person who created the character can always draw it better than you can. When you make contact with a professional, share your own characters. If you're good, they'll be impressed with your originality, and they'll appreciate your respect for their work.

HAVE YOU SEEN MILLS'S WORK?

Mills obviously learned from that early mistake and went on to use his artistic talent in a variety of exciting ways. After a stint drawing pictures of toys for a major toy company, Mills went to Hollywood and started working for an animation production company.

Did you see the movie *An American Tail*? Remember the scene when Fievel and his father are talking about fish as they sail to America from Russia? Mills helped do the drawings for that scene. Perhaps you're more familiar with the names Wacko, Yakko, and Dot? Mills is a five-time Emmy Award-winning producer, director, and animator of some of the hilarious shows, *Pinky and the Brain*, and *Animaniacs*. Mills also got a shot at producing, designing, and animating a show based on his own idea for Playhouse Disney. Even though the show didn't get picked up, he says that it was great experience working on his own project.

WELCOME TO THE REAL WORLD

The day he got out of art school, Mills thought he'd have a job like the one he has now. Surprise! Fourteen years later, he's made it to where he wants to be. But like most professions, animation is a field in which you have to work your way up, prove yourself, and learn all you can about the process of making animated films.

BEHIND THE SCENES IN HOLLYWOOD

The pace is fast, and the schedule is everything. Mills has learned to discipline himself to get the job done—whether he feels like it or not. This particular trick of the trade is true for anyone who hopes to succeed in this environment.

Mills has learned something else while working with big-name stars: they are all just regular people. This fact brings him back to earth when he starts taking himself too seriously. It also reminds him that anybody who's willing to do the hard work can be part of the seemingly glamorous world of Hollywood.

WHERE DO ALL THOSE WILD IDEAS COME FROM?

Coming up with a steady flow of creative story lines for shows like *Pinky and the Brain* and *Animaniacs* is a group effort. It starts with a staff of writers who meet regularly to discuss ideas. The eventual result of all their brainstorming is a script. At this point, the show's producers and directors jump in and make changes before accepting or rejecting the stories.

As supervising producer, Mills's job is to make sure that all the pieces fit. Whether it's the story itself, the background music, or the animation, he has to make sure that all the creative energy flows in the same direction.

NO EXCUSES

You don't have to starve to be an artist. There are plenty of ways to use artistic talent to make a good living. The opportunities are out there if you are willing to work hard and stick with it.

Architect

WHAT IS AN ARCHITECT?

"Architecture is the imaginative blend of art and science in the design of environments for people." That's how the American Institute of Architects defines architecture.

Basically, what this means is that architects design buildings, homes, and other structures that people use for work, play, and everyday life. These include churches, hospitals,

airports, industrial complexes, and even entire communities. Architects use art and their creativity to dream up structures that are visually appealing. Everyone can appreciate a beautiful house or an imposing office building.

Looks are important but they aren't the only aspect of design that an architect must confront. An architect must also make sure that the buildings he or she designs will actually stand up. This is where science comes into play. All those laws of physics and mathematics are applied in very important ways to make sure that structures can withstand the test of time. The architect's knowledge of math and science must be applied to details such as air-conditioning, heating and ventilating systems, electrical systems, and plumbing.

In addition, there are many legal issues to add to the equation. Architects must incorporate building codes, environmental concerns, fire regulations, and easy access for disabled people into the design process. They need to consider the wear and tear the building will be subject to by people using a structure day in and day out. And they must factor in an ample number of bathrooms and fire exits. They must also take precautions to insure a structure's ability to hold up to weather-related disasters, such as tornadoes and hurricanes.

With such a tall order to fill, architects need a fairly extensive education. The education process can be summed up in three steps. The first step is getting a five- to eight-year college education in architecture. College will include courses in art, engineering, history, and planning. The second step is to complete a paid internship with a certified architect that usually lasts three years. The final step is to complete a four-day exam to become a certified architect.

If you think you'd like to become an architect, make sure to take as many classes as you can in art and science. The American Association of Architects suggests that it's also important to cultivate an ability to see an object in space, a pattern, a method, a process, or a plan. Mathematical ability and drawing skills are definite pluses for the budding architect. It sounds rigorous, but it can be very rewarding if the idea of blending scientific laws with your own creative ideas appeals to you.

 **TRY IT OUT**

TAKE A HIKE!

One of the easiest ways to learn about architecture is to look around. Open your eyes and start to notice all the details in the buildings in your neighborhood. Go for a walk downtown and jot notes (or sketch diagrams) about the buildings you find most interesting. What features make them notable?

Compare various schools, stores, churches, and other buildings that you frequent. Start looking for those details that give each structure an identity. Think about the how and why elements behind each aspect of the design. What would you have done differently if you had been the architect in charge?

ARCHITECTURE 101

What makes a Victorian home Victorian? What elements are always found in a Classical structure? The following activity will help you answer questions like this and will provide an introduction to some architectural basics.

Divide a notebook into sections allowing separate space for a variety of architectural styles. Make sure to include styles such as Victorian, Classical, Gothic, Roman, Greek Revival, and Renaissance. Use the library and online search engines to find out all you can about each of these architectural styles (and others as you discover them). Write a description of all the elements that make each style unique. Include pictures or your drawings of identifying features. Whenever possible, include samples of famous buildings designed in each style.

 **CHECK IT OUT**

🖱 ON THE WEB

ONLINE ARCHITECTURE

Build upon your knowledge of architecture at these Web sites:

- 💡 Architects at a Glance at http://www.loggia.com/ designarts/architecture/bio/masterbiography.html

☼ Architecture for Children at http://www.archkidecture.org
☼ Architecture through the Ages at
  http://library.thinkquest.org/10098
☼ Building Big at http://www.pbs.org/wgbh/buildingbig
☼ Building of America at http://www.pbs.org/greatprojects

AT THE LIBRARY

BUILD IT AND THEY WILL COME

There's no better way to understand the architectural process than to build something from the ground up. The following books provide the ideas and instructions you'll need to get started:

Haslam, Andrew. *Building: Make It Work.* Minnetonka, Minn.: Two-Can, 2002.

Johmann, Carol. *Bridges: Amazing Structures to Design, Build, and Test.* Nashville, Tenn.: Williamson, 1999.

RESOURCES FOR THE YOUNG ARCHITECT

For a chance to learn some fascinating facts about architecture and to have some fun testing your architectural skills, take a look at the following books:

Bardhan-Quallen, Supidta. *The Eiffel Tower: Great Structures in History.* Farmington Hills, Mich.: Kidhaven Press, 2005. (Also look for other titles in the *Great Structures in History* series.)

Curlee, Lynn. *Seven Wonders of the Ancient World.* New York: Atheneum, 2002.

Hopkinson. *Sky Boys: How They Built the Empire State Building.* New York: Schwartz and Wade, 2006.

Issacson, Phillip. *Round Buildings, Square Buildings, and Buildings that Wiggle Like a Fish.* New York: Random House, 2001.

Lusted, Marcia. *The National Mall: Building History.* Farmington Hills, Mich.: Lucent, 2005. (Also, check out other titles in the *Building History* series.)

Maccauley, David. *Building Big.* New York: Houghton Mifflin, 2000.

Seymour, Simon. *Bridges.* San Francisco, Calif.: Chronicle, 2005.

Sullivan, George. *Build to Last: Building America's Bridges, Dams, Tunnels, and Skyscrapers.* New York: Scholastic, 2005.

If you can't find them at your local library or you'd like to obtain your own copy, these books and many other exceptionally good resources for students are available through the American Institute of Architects at 1735 New York Avenue NW, Washington, D.C. 20006-5292 or online at http://aia.org.

🗣️ WITH THE EXPERTS

American Institute of Architects
1735 New York Avenue NW
Washington, DC 20006-5292
http://www.aia.org

Association of Collegiate Schools of Architecture
1735 New York Avenue NW, 3rd Floor
Washington, DC 20006-5292
http://www.acsa-arch.org

Society for Architectural Historians
1365 North Astor Street
Chicago, IL 60610-2144
http://www.sah.org

GET ACQUAINTED

Michael Graves, Architect

CAREER PATH

CHILDHOOD ASPIRATION: To be an artist (ever since he was six years old).

FIRST JOB: Got his start working for an architectural firm in Cincinnati while he was going to college there.

CURRENT JOB: Architect and product designer, and professor recently retired from Princeton University.

OFF TO A GOOD START

Even as a child, Michael Graves showed talent as an artist. As a young boy, he loved to draw. Luckily for him, his mother recognized his talent and helped him channel it into an artistic profession. She suspected that it would be hard to make a living as an artist, so she suggested architecture or engineering. Engineering was a bit too technical for Graves, so he set his sights on architecture.

ONE OF A KIND

The *New York Times* calls Graves "the most truly original voice that American architecture has produced in some time." That's quite a compliment. Early in his career, Graves was credited with starting a movement in architecture called postmodernism, but he didn't just stop there. He has kept on creating architecture that blends traditional and contemporary forms and that feels like it belongs in its context of surrounding buildings. His floor plans and the spaces he designs are orderly and often use symmetry to help organize them. He prefers warm, "livable" designs that make people feel at home.

FROM TOWERS TO TEAKETTLES

Graves has lent his creative touch to projects big and small, from giant hotels at places like Walt Disney World and towers in New York City to teakettles and tabletop items. His penchant for designing "things" as well as "places" began soon after getting his second architecture degree, from Harvard University. He worked for a firm in New York that specialized in consumer product design in addition to building design. Product design continues to be a major part of his firm's work; they have designed nearly 2,000 products. You can find some of these products in the Michael Graves collection featured in the housewares department of your local Target store.

A WORLDWIDE INFLUENCE

Japan, China, Korea, Taiwan, Costa Rica, Mexico, Egypt, Belgium, and Holland are among the many places where Graves's work stands abroad. Closer to home in the United States, you might want to look at some of these works of art:

- Denver Central Library in Denver
- Clark County Library and Theater in Las Vegas
- Alexandria Public Library in Alexandria, Virginia
- U.S. Courthouse in Washington, D.C.
- Swan and Dolphin Hotels at Walt Disney World in Orlando, Florida
- Team Disney Building in Burbank, California
- 425 Fifth Avenue (residential tower) in New York City
- The Newark Museum in Newark, New Jersey
- Minneapolis Institute of Art and Children's Theatre in Minneapolis
- The Detroit Institute of Arts in Detroit
- Michael C. Carlos Museum at Emory University in Atlanta
- NCAA Headquarters and Hall of Champions in Indianapolis, Indiana
- The Humana Building in Louisville, Kentucky
- Engineering Research Center at the University of Cincinnati in Cincinnati
- Miele's headquarters in Princeton, New Jersey

- ☀ Martel College at Rice University in Houston, Texas
- ☀ NovaCare Complex, Philadelphia Eagles Training Center in Philadelphia

If you don't live anywhere near these places, you can get a sneak peek at a variety of Graves's works in books such as *Michael Graves Buildings and Projects: 1990–1994* or *Michael Graves Buildings and Projects: 1995-2003* (New York: Rizzoli, 1995 and 2003, respectively). Or visit Graves's Web site at http://www.michaelgraves.com.

IF HE WERE YOUR AGE . . .

Graves says that one of the most important things that a young person considering a career in architecture can do is to get curious—about his or her surroundings, historic buildings, new structures, and other tangible evidences of modern life. He says that good architects study the buildings of ancient Rome as well as the high-rises of modern Chicago. By seeing how buildings and styles have changed over time, architects see how our culture has changed.

He also recommends pursuing a well-rounded education—starting now. Take courses such as history, literature, art, and philosophy to become aware of political and social events as well as social trends. Becoming an avid reader of books, magazines, and newspapers is also crucial to learning how to build for people and the world in which they live.

HIT THE ROAD

Travel is another effective way to build awareness. For instance, an aspiring architect can compare the similarities and differences between Japanese and American houses by traveling through both countries. Graves recommends that architects visit different countries and regions as much as possible.

A FINAL WORD

Graves works from the premise that the past, the present, and the future are part of the same chain. By studying the past and present, an architect can design buildings that will be part of the future.

Artist

SHORTCUTS

GO visit art galleries and museums.

READ about famous artists such as Michelangelo, Mary Cassatt, and Claude Monet.

TRY experimenting with various types of art to find your niche.

SKILL SET

✔ ART

✔ BUSINESS

✔ TALKING

WHAT IS AN ARTIST?

What's the first thing that comes to mind when you think about an "artist"? Does it involve someone painting scenes at the seashore while wearing a funny-looking hat and balancing a palette of paints? That's one of the many stereotypes often associated with the world of art.

The reality is that there are countless ways to make art the centerpiece of a rewarding career. An artist is someone who uses creative expression to produce works of art. The results of their work can exist simply for giving pleasure to others in mediums such as painting and sculpture. Or their work may serve both an aesthetic and a functional purpose. This means that their work

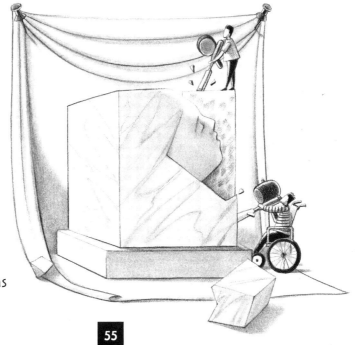

not only looks good but can also be used in a practical way. Examples are greeting cards, pottery, or jewelry.

Whatever the artistic medium, whether it be watercolors or weaving, all artists must make certain decisions in order to avoid another stereotype: the starving artist syndrome. An important goal of all careers is to make money, but for most artists, relying on their creative talent is not always sufficient to achieve this goal. That's where good business sense and strong communication skills can come in handy.

In order to make money, artists must find someone willing to pay for their work. Some artists do this through commercial methods, working for a company noted for producing and distributing various kinds of products. Others offer their work through art galleries, museums, and retail shops. This method involves some legwork in order to find an ongoing source of space to show their work. Sometimes it takes an entrepreneurial twist to push an artist into the ranks of the comfortably self-sufficient.

This was certainly the case for one very talented painter. His work was good, but he just couldn't seem to sell enough of his works to stay afloat. He needed to do something else, but he knew that he'd never be happy doing something that didn't utilize his artistic skill. After thinking things over, he had a great idea. Instead of painting on canvas, he started painting on clothes—sweatshirts, jogging shorts, etc. He found some upscale boutiques to sell these items for him. When the orders started coming faster than he could paint them, he knew he was on to something.

The lesson here is that sometimes artists have to apply some of their creative energy to creating profitable avenues for their art. That element adds all kinds of interesting possibilities to the mix.

There really are no specific educational requirements for being an artist. It goes without saying that talent is the number-one prerequisite. Natural artistic ability is not something that can be taught—you either have it or you don't. The second most important prerequisite is an exciting portfolio to showcase your experience and best efforts.

That second prerequisite makes many artists realize the need for advanced education. Even some of the most talented artists discover that pursuing a bachelor's or graduate degree in an area such as fine arts or art history adds a new, more developed and refined dimension to their artwork. Formal education is, of course, a must for those who want to teach or work in a museum.

Aspiring artists, take heart. Opportunities abound for those willing to work hard, perfect their craft, and look for creative ways to bridge the gap between starving artist and thriving artist.

 **TRY IT OUT**

KEEP A RUNNING LIST

Widen your artistic horizons by filling a notebook with all the different ways people make a living with their art. Start with some of the traditional methods such as painting, pottery, and weaving.

Keep your eyes open and add articles and descriptions of other creative outlets for artistic expression. For example, one artist in Arizona used the clay-colored dirt that is native to his region to color unusual T-shirts and other fashions. Another artist created Impressionist-style paintings of her clients' favorite photographs.

The possibilities are endless!

JUST DO ART!

Take advantage of every opportunity you can find to make art. Seek opportunities to experiment with as many different mediums as you can. Use watercolors and pastels. Try clay and various textiles. Put mediums together in unusual ways. Doing this serves two purposes: You continue to perfect your skills, and you discover areas that make the most of your unique artistic talents.

Some of the ways to do this include taking art classes at school or through your community's continuing education program and signing up for classes in art studios or at art museums.

THE REST OF THE STORY

Everyday life offers plenty of opportunities for creative expression. Take a sketchpad to the mall, airport, or park and find a comfortable spot to sit and observe. Watch as people interact with each other and with the environment. Sketch what you see in a series of scenes (something like a comic strip layout) and embellish each scene with your own ideas for the story behind the story. For instance, make up a story about the two people whom you saw embracing emotionally at the airport.

Another idea is actually to illustrate scenes from a favorite chapter book of yours.

CHECK IT OUT

ON THE WEB

ARTIST ONLINE

Learn, explore museums, and just goof off at some of the following art-inspired Web sites:

- ☼ ArtCyclopeida at http://www.artcyclopedia.com
- ☼ Scribbles Kids Art Site at http://www.scribbleskidsart. com
- ☼ Arts Connected at http://www.artsconnected.org
- ☼ Destination Modern Art at http://www.moma.org/ destination
- ☼ National Gallery of Art Kids at http://www.nga.gov/kids
- ☼ Museum Kids at http://www.metmuseum.org/ explore/museumkids.htm

AT THE LIBRARY

TAKE A CRASH COURSE IN ART HISTORY

Serious artists know who's who in the art world. You can learn a lot from other successful artists, especially those whose work has stood the test of time. Michelangelo, Leonardo da Vinci, and Vincent van Gogh are just a few of the artists who continue to enjoy worldwide fame even centuries after they completed their works. Do yourself a favor and bone up on some of these great artists. Following are some suggested resources to make this task enjoyable and easy:

Cole, Alison. *Eyewitness: Renaissance.* New York: DK Publishing, 2000.

Fry, Frieda. *Frida Kahlo: The Artist Who Painted Herself.* New York: Grosset and Dunlap, 2003

Holulb, Joan. *Vincent van Gogh: Sunflowers and Swirlys.* New York: Grosset and Dunlap, 2001.

Kelly, Tina. *Pablo Picasso: Breaking All the Rules.* New York: Grosset and Dunlap, 2001.

Langley, Andrew. *DaVinci and His Times.* New York: DK Publishing, 2006.

O'Connor, Jane. *Edgar Degas: Paintings That Dance.* New York: Grosset and Dunlap, 2001.

———. *Henri Matisse: Drawing with Scissors.* New York: Grosset and Dunlap, 2002.

———. *Mary Cassatt: Family Pictures.* New York: Grosset and Dunlap, 2003.

O'Reilly, Wanda, and Erin Kravitz. *The Renaissance Art Book: Discover 30 Glorious Masterpieces by Leonardo da Vinci, Michelangelo, Raphael, Fra Angelico, and Botticelli.* Palo Alto, Calif.: Birdcage Press, 2001.

Welton, Jude. *Eyewitness: Impressionism.* New York: DK Publishing, 2000.

For information about women artists contact the National Museum of Women in the Arts, 1250 New York Avenue NW, Washington, D.C., 20005-3920, or go online to http://nmwa.org.

FUN STUFF FOR ARTISTS

Just for fun, jump into some of the artistic mystery and mayhem featured in the following books:

Balliett, Blue. *Chasing Vermeer.* New York: Scholastic, 2004.

Cressy, Judith. *Can You Find It? Search and Discover More Than 150 Details in 19 Works of Art.* New York: Henry Abrams, 2002.

————. *Can You Find It, Too? Search and Discover More Than 150 Details in 20 Works of Art.* New York: Henry Abrams, 2004.

Nilsen, Anna. *Art Fraud Detective: Spot the Difference, Solve the Crime.* New York: Kingfisher, 2000.

————. *The Great Art Scandal: Solve the Crime, Save the Show.* New York: Kingfisher, 2003.

📣 WITH THE EXPERTS

Allied Artists of America
15 Gramercy Park South
New York, NY 10003-1705
http://alliedartistsofamerica.org

American Art Therapy
  Association
1202 Allanson Road
Mundelein, IL 60060-3808
http://arttherapy.org

American Crafts Council
72 Spring Street
New York, NY 10012-4019
http://craftcouncil.org

National Art Education
  Association
1916 Association Drive
Reston, VA 20191-1502
http://www.naea-reston.org

National Endowment for the
  Arts
1100 Pennsylvania Avenue NW
Washington, DC 20506-0001
http://www.nea.gov

GET ACQUAINTED

Mary Engelbreit, Artist

CAREER PATH

CHILDHOOD ASPIRATION:
To illustrate children's books.

FIRST JOB: Working full-time
at an art supply store.

CURRENT JOB: "Queen" of
Mary Engelbreit, INK.

AUNT JEMIMA, BETTY CROCKER, AND MARY ENGELBREIT?

Not many people reach such a high level of success that their very name conjures up the image of a beloved product. For Aunt Jemima, it's pancakes and syrup. For Betty Crocker, it's cake mixes and cookbooks. For Mary Engelbreit, it's greeting cards, children's books, calendars, and hundreds of other charming products, all bearing her one-of-a-kind signature style.

The thing that makes Engelbreit different from the others is that she is a real person (sorry to break the news, but the other two are just marketing gimmicks). She is the creative force behind a company that has grown into a "mini-empire," with millions of avid collectors all over the world.

The people who know her best describe her as whimsical, nostalgic, playful, optimistic, and a bit irreverent. That's exactly how her fans would describe her art, too!

IT DIDN'T HAPPEN OVERNIGHT

According to Engelbreit's mother, her daughter was drawing from the time she could pick up a pencil. By the time she was 11, Engelbreit had talked her mother into converting a linen closet into her very own art studio. She started out re-creating pictures from old storybooks (Johnny Gruelle's Raggedy Ann and Andy books were early favorites). She admits that she taught herself to draw by copying but says that if you copy something long enough, pretty soon you'll start drawing your own stuff just as well.

Later she began drawing pictures of scenes from favorite books such as *The Secret Garden*, *Jane Eyre*, *The Little Princess*, and the *Nancy Drew* series.

IN THE "YOU KNOW YOU'VE MADE IT BIG WHEN" CATEGORY

One of the artists that Engelbreit most admired was Joan Walsh Anglund. Anglund was among the first to introduce small, richly illustrated gift books filled with short, inspirational sayings. Even as a child, Engelbreit realized that this concept was something she could do as an artist. Now, some 30 years later, she is amazed (and very pleased) to find her own little books sitting on bookstore shelves right next to Anglund's. It marks one of those telling moments when desire and destiny intersect and make life come full circle. Maybe it sounds dramatic, but it happens to everyone at one point or another.

DON'T TELL ANYONE, BUT . . .

Even though Engelbreit had the potential to be an excellent student, she really didn't like school very much. By the time she made it through high school, she was ready to get out of school for good and get to work. In her mind, there was only one thing she wanted to do, and that was to illustrate children's books. That she had no idea how to find paying work illustrating children's books was no deterrent.

Instead of college, Engelbreit embarked on a self-taught discovery of the world of art, and she credits several experiences for broadening her horizons. The first was her job at the art supply store. It was there that she discovered that there are many ways to make a living while making art. The next step was illustrating ads for a very small advertising agency. It was there that she learned about the business of art.

A transition into freelance illustration kept Engelbreit busy illustrating posters, ads, newspapers, and magazine editorials. However, she never lost sight of what she really wanted to do: illustrate children's books.

Later, her husband persuaded a friend in publishing to arrange some interviews with art directors. So Engelbreit put together a portfolio and took off for New York, certain that everyone would be eager to have her illustrate their books. But, much to her disappointment, no one jumped at the chance to put her to work. The last art director advised her to consider illustrating greeting cards.

A little insulted at first, it turns out that this advice became an important turning point in Engelbreit's career. That's because she took the advice and started producing greeting cards for other publishers. The cards were so successful that she started her own company and expanded her line to include other products.

In fact, it was her success in greeting cards that finally brought the opportunity to illustrate a children's book, an updated version of *The Snow Queen*, as well as a series of decorating, gardening, and crafts books and a whole line of gift books.

She now has a long-term contract to illustrate more than 20 new children's books, including classics like *The Night Before Christmas and Mother Goose*, plus original stories she will also write about her alter ego character Ann Estelle. *The Night Before Christmas* has already been turned into an animated home video, bringing her drawings to life for the first time. She has plans for many more children's books and animated videos. As Ann Estelle once said, "Imagine the possibilities!"

READ ALL ABOUT HER!

Chances are you can walk into any greeting card store in America and find samples of Engelbreit's work. Some find her work to be very addicting! Once you discover it, you might get hooked!

Another way to find out more about her work is to read the book *Mary Engelbreit: The Art and the Artist* (Kansas City, Mo.: Andrews and McMeel, 1996). It includes examples of her earliest drawings as well as those that have brought her the most acclaim. It also offers a lively description of her journey as an artist and businesswoman.

Also, she has available a special Web page and packet for aspiring artists. Visit the "for artists" section of her Web site at http://www.maryengelbreit.com or send a self-addressed, stamped envelope to Mary Engelbreit INK, 1001 Highlands Plaza Drive West, Suite 450, St. Louis, MO 63110-1337.

Chef

WHAT IS A CHEF?

Chefs are artists who express their creativity with foods. Chefs are highly trained culinary artists who learn to make food look as good as it tastes. People pay top dollar to enjoy chefs' innovative and visually appealing dishes.

Chefs work in some of the finest restaurants in the world, as well as in corporate facilities, resorts, and other places where fine food is offered. Some chefs run their own catering companies and provide fancy menus at occasions such as weddings, sporting events, and black-tie affairs. For others, the ultimate symbol of success is owning their own restaurants.

Some of the better-known chefs publish their own cookbooks and host their own cooking shows on television. Others share selected trade secrets at upscale cooking classes or in magazine articles.

The work of chefs tends to be highly specialized with several kinds of chefs often presiding over specific areas of a busy kitchen. These specialties include

chef de froid, who designs and prepares decorated foods and artistic food arrangements for buffets in formal restaurants. This work can include making ice sculptures, molding butter into unusual designs, and decorating food trays using colorful fruits and vegetables.

executive chef, who takes charge of the total "back of the house," or kitchen operation. This chef supervises other chefs and manages the ordering and receiving of all food supplies. He or she also deals with management issues such as hiring, costs, quality, and product development.

pastry chef, who supervises and coordinates activities of cooks preparing pastries, desserts, ice cream, and other confections. This chef also makes pastry and table decorations using sugar paste and icings.

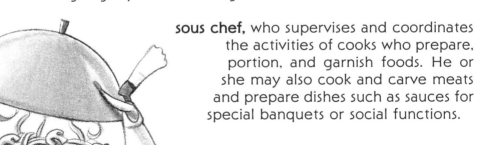

sous chef, who supervises and coordinates the activities of cooks who prepare, portion, and garnish foods. He or she may also cook and carve meats and prepare dishes such as sauces for special banquets or social functions.

To become a chef, you must earn at least an associate's degree in culinary arts. A good program covers topics such as American and international cuisines, nutrition,

menu planning, customer relations, and some basic management issues. Any good program will also include extensive
hands-on training in food preparation techniques. An internship experience, where you get the chance to put your newfound skills to work in the kitchen of a busy restaurant, is also
an important part of the training process.

You may also want to consider pursuing a bachelor's degree
in culinary arts management. The degree takes four years and
provides more intensive training and preparation for the management side of things.

Since the experts project that jobs in the food and hospital-
ity industry are expected to increase over the next several
years, a good chef can expect a wide range of jobs from
which to choose. If you have any doubts about that predic-
tion, just look up all the restaurant listings in the yellow pages
of any good-sized town, and you'll see that the possibilities for
good chefs are nearly endless.

 TRY IT OUT

WHAT'S FOR COOKING?

Your family's kitchen is a great place to test your desire to be a
chef. Just step in and start cooking. Begin with the cookbooks you
find there and cook foods that your family normally enjoys.

Branch out by borrowing different kinds of cookbooks from
the library and planning some interesting new menus. Make a list
of the ingredients and ask if you can tag along on the next trip
to the grocery store. Be sure to follow the directions carefully.

Make it a point to serve your meals with style. Use the nicest
dishes (that your parents will allow), set the table, and maybe
even add some candlelight and soft music. Remember that
chefs have two goals when preparing food: making it taste
good and making it look good. So, practice different presenta-
tion techniques and arrange the food nicely on each plate.

For an extra challenge, make a chart with space for each
day in the week. Plan a complete dinner menu for seven
days in a row. Include choices sure to please each member
of your family and foods that represent each of the five food

groups (grains, vegetables, fruits, milk, and meat and beans) included in the food pyramid. See http://www.mypyramid.gov for an interactive introduction.

CHOCOLATE FEST

It's a chocolate lover's dream come true! You are the designated chef for a party where everything on the menu will feature chocolate as a main ingredient. Use cookbooks and online resources to plan a menu and gather recipes. You'll find some mouth-watering ideas at Web sites that include:

- ☀ http://www.hersheys.com/kidztown
- ☀ http://www.m-ms.com/us/baking/recipes/
- ☀ http://www.fieldmuseum.org/chocolate/kids_recipes.html
- ☀ http://www.homeschoolzone.com/m2m/chocolate.htm

TV DINNER

Thanks to cable television you can now visit the kitchens of some of the world's most renowned chefs. Go online to http://www.foodtv.com to check local listings of the food network's delectable selection of shows.

Keep some 3 x 5 cards handy when you watch your favorite chefs in action so you can jot down some of their tips and techniques. Label each card with the chef's name and the name and time of the show. Include just one tip per card and in no time you'll have compiled a mini-library of expert cooking advice.

 CHECK IT OUT

 ON THE WEB

CLIMB THE FOOD PYRAMID

The United States Dairy Association has spent a lot of time (and your parents' tax dollars) figuring out what healthy people need to eat and has created the "food pyramid" to describe a nutritious diet. If you know what's good for you as a future chef, you'll get acquainted with these guidelines. The following Web sites will help you get started.

- ☼ See http://www.mypyramid.gov for an interactive introduction to the food pyramid.
- ☼ Play the Food Pyramid Game at http://www. hooah4health.com/body/nutrition/ pyramidinteractive.htm.
- ☼ Take a Food Pyramid challenge at http://www. kidskonnect.com/FoodPyramid/FoodPyramidHome. html.

ONLINE CHEF

There is a terrific Web site on the Internet called Online Chef. It includes interviews with famous chefs, menus, interesting new recipes, a glossary of food jargon, cooking tips and techniques, and all kinds of interesting articles. It's free and it's fun. Check it out at http://www.onlinechef.com.

PLAY WITH YOUR FOOD

It's a cyber buffet of fun food Web sites! Go online and chow down on some of these fun resources.

- ☼ Find games tips and quizzes at www.coolfoodplantet. org.
- ☼ Get friendly with some fruits and veggies at http:// www.dole5aday.com/.
- ☼ Check the Kid's Health Web site at http://www.kid-shealth.org/kid/.
- ☼ Stop by the Nutrition Café at http://www.exhibits. pacsci.org/nutrition/nutrition_cafe.html.
- ☼ Go to http://www.kidchef.com, where kids rule the kitchen.
- ☼ Take a virtual trip to the late Julia Child's kitchen at http://americanhistory.si.edu/juliachild.
- ☼ Find all kinds of kid-friendly cooking resources at http://www.thelovechef.com/kids.

And, last but definitely not least, don't miss all the excitement included in these two sites:

- ☼ Smart Mouth at http://www.cspinet.org/cgi-bin/smartmouth/choose.pl
- ☼ Your Energy Wake Up Call at http://www.caprojectlean.org

 AT THE LIBRARY

EAT YOUR WAY AROUND THE WORLD

Explore the world's cuisine in some of the following books:

Buller, Laura. *Eyewitness: Food.* New York: DK Publishing, 2005.

Parks, Peggy. *Foods of France: Taste of Culture.* Farmington Hills, Mich.: KidHaven, 2005.

Sheen, Barbara. *Foods of China: Taste of Culture.* Farmington Hills, Mich.: KidHaven, 2006.

———. *Foods of Greece: Taste of Culture.* Farmington Hills, Mich.: KidHaven, 2005.

———. *Foods of Italy: Taste of Culture.* Farmington Hills, Mich.: KidHaven, 2005.

———. *Foods of Japan: Taste of Culture.* Farmington Hills, Mich.: KidHaven, 2005.

———. *Foods of Mexico: Taste of Culture.* Farmington Hills, Mich.: KidHaven, 2005.

When you're ready to take the plunge as amateur chef, try some of the international ideas found in:

Gioffre, Rosalba. *The Young Chef's French Cookbook.* New York: Crabtree, 2001.

———. *The Young Chef's Italian Cookbook.* New York: Crabtree, 2001.

Lee, Frances. *The Young Chef's Chinese Cookbook.* New York: Crabtree, 2001.

Ward, Karen. *The Young Chef's Mexican Cookbook.* New York: Crabtree, 2001.

If all that cooking has you wanting more, consider making the culinary arts a career with advice found in the following book:

Englart, Mindi. *How Do I Become a Chef?* Farmington Hills, Mich.: Blackbirch Press, 2002.

A SCIENTIST IN THE KITCHEN

Cook up some science experiments with some of the ideas described in the following books:

Parson, Russ. *How to Read a French Fry and Other Stories of Intriguing Kitchen Science.* New York: Houghton Mifflin, 2003.

Wolke. Robert. *What Einstein Told His Cook: Kitchen Science Explained.* New York: W.W. Norton, 2002.

————. *What Einstein Told His Cook 2: Further Adventures in Kitchen Science.* New York: W.W. Norton, 2005.

🗣 WITH THE EXPERTS

For more information on opportunities for chefs, contact

American Culinary Federation
180 Center Place Way
St. Augustine, FL 32095-8859
http://www.acfchefs.org

Council on Hotel, Restaurant and Institution Education
2810 North Parham Road, Suite 230
Richmond, VA 23294-4434
http://www.chrie.org

National Restaurant Association
Educational Foundation
175 West Jackson Boulevard, Suite 1500
Chicago, IL 60604-2814
http://www.nraef.org

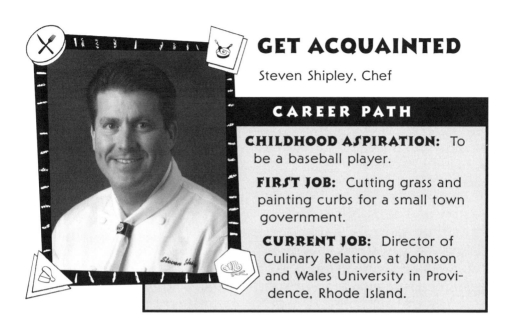

GET ACQUAINTED

Steven Shipley, Chef

CAREER PATH

CHILDHOOD ASPIRATION: To be a baseball player.

FIRST JOB: Cutting grass and painting curbs for a small town government.

CURRENT JOB: Director of Culinary Relations at Johnson and Wales University in Providence, Rhode Island.

Steven Shipley often gives talks to groups of students. He says that walking into a room wearing a tall white hat and white jacket is a surefire way to get their attention. He tells these groups that becoming a chef is one way to work your way around the world. He tells them that restaurants aren't the only place where chefs work. Chefs also work at spas and resorts like Disney World, in war zones, on aircraft carriers for the military, in universities and hospitals. Working in the homes and aboard the yachts of the rich and famous is where some chefs find employment, while others feed the masses attending major sporting events and celebrations like the Olympics or Super Bowl.

COOKING UP A CAREER

Shipley's career in food got its start at a Pizza Hut in Hershey, Pennsylvania. While working there he and a friend took a road trip to Rhode Island to visit the campus of Johnson and Wales which, at the time, had one of only three culinary training programs in the United States. He enrolled in the program and has enjoyed a nonstop culinary career ever since.

During summer breaks from classes he dressed in a tuxedo and worked as a table-side chef entertaining guests at a hotel by making dishes like steak Diane and bananas flambé. Next on his career menu was a stint working as a chef for a yacht club on the Long Island Sound. This job included housing provided by the club and allowed him to gain experience as a "chef tournant," or a chef who works all the positions. There he prepared food for special events like seafood buffets and special ethnic theme nights.

After graduating from culinary school, he temporarily traded in the chef's hat for a suit and tie to work as a chef consultant with a company that managed on-site employee cafeterias for Harley Davidson, a shoe manufacturer, banks, and a major health insurance company. His territory included a 200-mile radius in central Pennsylvania, and his job was to help the on-site chefs with tasks like setting up menus, food preparing, and planning events. At one event, for a pharmaceutical company, he devised a system for feeding 600 employees in just 15 minutes!

Next came an 18-month stint in Lafayette, Louisiana, where he learned how to spice up his cooking Cajun- and Creole-style. He admits that it took a while for him to get used to this version of "seasoned" food—which he initially described as "blowing my head off spicy." Ultimately, he really enjoyed the exposure to a different and utterly fascinating culture.

A LITTLE OF THIS, A LITTLE OF THAT

Shipley's career continued along an interesting track from there. He was offered a position teaching other chefs at Johnson and Wales, which he continued during the school year for six years. During summers off from teaching he worked as a private chef in an 11-bedroom, oceanfront home on Cape Cod. It was his job to pamper an onslaught of guests who were already so pampered that they arrived by helicopter.

Later in his career, he was back in a suit and tie working with a Manhattan-based food service consulting company that specialized in hospitals, schools, stadiums, and universities. Weekends were reserved for catering special events in Westchester County.

Before returning to Johnson and Wales in his current position, he also worked as chef for a New York City law firm.

ADVICE AL DENTE

With all that experience under his belt, Shipley says two practices have helped him build a solid reputation as a chef: when he makes a commitment he sticks to it, and he makes it a habit to return phone calls and emails.

Other than that, he warns that the field is completely addictive in a wonderful way. He's found it a fascinating industry with endless opportunity to learn something new every day, see the world, and surround yourself with interesting people.

Choreographer

WHAT IS A CHOREOGRAPHER?

Dancing is where almost all choreographers get their start. It's not at all unusual for professional dancers to start learning their future profession when they are five or six years old. Most dancers have begun to show a serious interest (and the talent to match) by their early teens. That's not to say that it's impossible to get started any later; it's just unusual.

A dancer acquires self-discipline and physical stamina by faithfully adhering to a regimen of dance lessons and rehearsals throughout his or her young years. These attributes are absolutely essential for making it as a professional dancer. And, making it as a professional dancer is the standard prerequisite for becoming a choreographer. Since one of the main functions of a choreographer's job is to invent dances, it makes sense that a choreographer needs plenty of dance experience to do that.

Choreographers are dance makers. They create patterns of movement and arrange steps or sequences of movement in such a way that they tell a story, make a statement, or express an emotion. As inventors of new and exciting forms of movement, they are always looking for unusual ways to put movement, steps, and music together. Quite often the choreographer must act like a matchmaker,

arranging a perfect marriage between a musical composition and its interpretation in dance. In simplest terms, a choreographer's job consists of three parts:

- ☿ creating steps and movement to fit a particular purpose or musical selection
- ☿ teaching dancers how to perform the piece
- ☿ directing dancers during performances

Other, less obvious, requirements for the job include having excellent people and motivational skills. Knowing how to work well with people comes in very handy when dealing with the temperamental types who find their way into a production. The motivational skills are invaluable for encouraging top-notch performances out of dancers who have been touring for weeks and are running out of steam.

Dance itself is the most important training requirement for choreographers. Many colleges and universities offer excellent preparation for this profession through their physical education, music, theater, or fine arts departments. A well-rounded program will provide experience in music, theater, costuming, camera and editing techniques, and other aspects of creative art. Many programs also offer opportunities to gain experience in actually staging and participating in productions.

Some would argue that a formal education can be a detriment to a career in dance because it requires too much time away from actually performing. Many dancers find that training with the best possible dance instructors they can find helps prepare them for the rigors of professional dance. This route involves countless hours in dance studios, rehearsals, and private lessons learning techniques and practicing skills until they are absolutely flawless. Aspiring dancers should seek out advice from parents, trusted adults, and respected role models to determine the best ways to prepare themselves for a career in dance.

Choosing the best education and training is something that is worth serious consideration by anyone pursuing a career in dance. Whatever route you take, count on dance lessons, rehearsals, and lots of daily practice being a big part of your life. Martha Graham, one of America's most admired choreographers, defined dance as "the hidden language of the soul." To find out if dance is a part of your destiny, listen and see if it whispers your name.

☞ TRY IT OUT

FRIDAY NIGHT AT THE MOVIES

Dancers work in musical theater, film, and video, as well as in the ballet and concert field. You'll want to learn as much as you can about each of these forums for dance. Fortunately, there's a simple way to do this: Watch dancers dance. Go to concerts, watch the old musicals, see the newest moves in the latest music videos.

Make sure to watch films from every era: Start with some of the classics, starring Fred Astaire and Ginger Rogers, bop into the 1950s with *Grease*, and go disco-crazy with *Saturday Night Fever*. Pay special attention to how the dance scenes are choreographed. Feel free to dance along!

MAKE THE RIGHT MOVES

If you are absolutely new to the world of dance, you'll want to start with the basics. To get an insider's perspective on dance

positions, performance techniques, and various forms of dance, check out *The Young Dancer* by Darcy Bussell, with Patricia Linton (New York: DK Publishing, 1994) and *Eyewitness: Dance by Andree Grau* (New York: DK Publishing, 2005).

SHARE YOUR TALENT

Underneath all the glamor and hard work, choreography eventually boils down to one thing: teaching other dancers. Successful choreographers insure that the dancers understand not only the movements but also the mood and perspective behind each dance. This advanced teaching skill is acquired only through lots of practice and fully developed communication skills.

If you've been studying dance for a number of years, you may be ready to start sharing your skill with others. Talk to your dance instructors about helping teach classes for younger or less advanced students. Pour your heart into it, and you'll be rewarded every time one of your young protégés performs on stage.

DANCE MAKERS

Choreographers are professional dance makers. If you have access to a cassette or CD player and know some good moves, you have everything you need to become an amateur choreographer. Pick a favorite piece of music and invent a dance that expresses what you feel when you listen to it. Work on it. Revise and perfect. Keep going until you feel completely immersed in the music and movement. When you are ready, perform your dance for your family or a group of friends.

 CHECK IT OUT

ON THE WEB

DANCING IN CYBERSPACE

Following are a few exceptional Internet Web sites you can visit to learn more about choreography and other aspects of dance from these phenomenal dance studios:

☼ School of American Ballet at http://www.sab.org

- Alvin Ailey American Dance Theater at
  http://www.alvinailey.org
- The Joffrey Ballet School at
  http://www.joffreyballetschool.com
- Martha Graham School of Contemporary Dance at
  http://www.marthagrahamdance.org

You'll also find plenty to amaze and entertain you at these Web sites:

- Free to Dance at http://www.pbs.org/wnet/freetodance
- Great Dancers of the Twentieth Century at
  http://library.thinkquest.org/21702/lite/dance9.
  html?tqskip1=1&tqtime=0103
- The Ballet Encyclopedia at http://www.the-ballet.
  com/encyclopedia.php
- Virtual hamsters at http://www.hampsterdance.
  com/hampsterdanceredux.html
- The Web site for kids who love to dance at
  http://www.dance-kids.org

 AT THE LIBRARY

DANCERS TELL THEIR STORIES
Read the following dance-inspired stories:

Dowd, Olympia. *A Young Dancer's Apprenticeship.* Brookfield, Conn.: Millbrook Press, 2003.

Grover, Lorie Ann. *On Pointe.* New York: McElderberry, 2004.

Hon Goh, Chan. *Beyond the Dance: A Ballerina's Life.* Toronto, Ontario: Tundra Books, 2002.

Moss, Alexandra. *The Royal Ballet School Diaries.* New York: Grosset and Dunlap, 2005.

Porter, Tracey. *Dance of Sisters.* New York: Joanna Cutler, 2002.

READABLE ROLE MODELS

The following titles from the Library of American Chore-ographers will introduce you to some of the world's best choreographers:

Cady, Jennifer. *José Limón*. New York: Rosen, 2006.
Derezinski, Amelia. *Twyla Tharp*. New York: Rosen, 2005.
Gaskill, Rachel. *Agnes DeMille*. New York: Rosen, 2006.
Gitenstein, Judy. *Alvin Ailey*. New York: Rosen, 2006.
Kessey, Kristen. *Martha Graham*. New York: Rosen, 2006.
Seibert, Brian. *Jerome Robbins*. New York: Rosen, 2006.

WITH THE EXPERTS

American Dance Guild
PO Box 2006
Lenox Hill Station
New York, NY 10021
http://www.americandanceguild.org

Dance Notation Bureau
151 West 30th Street, Suite 202
New York, NY 10001-4007
http://dancenotation.org

Dance Theater Workshop
219 West 19th Street
New York, New York 10011-4001
http://www.dtw.org

Dance/USA
1156 15th Street NW, Suite 820
Washington, DC 20005-1704
http://www.danceusa.org

National Dance Association
1900 Association Drive
Reston, VA 20191-1502
http://www.aahperd.org/nda

Professional Dance Teachers Association
PO Box 38
Waldwick, NJ 07463

Society of Stage Directors and Choreographers
1501 Broadway, Suite 1701
New York, NY 10036-5601
http://www.ssdc.org

DANCING FOR A LIVING

The National Dance Association publishes a booklet called *Dance: A Career for You.* It describes various career opportunities for dancers including teacher, therapist, recreation leader, and, of course, choreographer. Request a free copy from the address listed earlier.

Once you've had a chance to read it over, make a chart listing each of the options with space to write down a comparison of the pros and cons of each.

GET ACQUAINTED

Judith Jamison, Choreographer, Dancer, Artistic Director

CAREER PATH

CHILDHOOD ASPIRATION: To be a dancer.

FIRST JOB: Teaching dance.

CURRENT JOB: Artistic director at the Alvin Ailey American Dance Theater.

BORN TO DANCE

According to her mother, Judith Jamison had a dancer's long legs and slender fingers even as a baby. She was so active

that she wore out a couple of cribs by jumping around in them constantly.

Fortunately, she never outgrew all that energy, and her wise mother helped her channel it into dancing when Jamison was just six years old. Dancing has been a major part of Jamison's life ever since. By age eight she was dancing on pointe and says that the shoes "felt like iron booties." At age 10, her teacher often used her to demonstrate proper dance combinations to classes full of adults. By the time she was 14, Jamison was teaching younger children with a focused determination that was well beyond her years.

BREAKING THE BARRIERS

Most dancers are female, petite, and white. Jamison is a woman, but she's a very tall African-American woman. As with anyone who goes against the status quo, she's had to work hard to prove herself and forge her own unique identity.

COLLISION WITH DESTINY

While Jamison was still a student at the Philadelphia Dance Academy, she went with some classmates to see a performance of the Alvin Ailey American Dance Theater. Watching the performance of Revelations, and inspired by one dancer in particular, Jamison was struck by the realization that "I can do that." Little did she know how closely her future would be linked with this famous dance company.

THE LUCKY BREAK

It was eight o'clock at night. Jamison had already taken five classes, and she was exhausted. Agnes de Mille (a legend in American dance) was on campus to teach a master class. (In a master class, someone who is especially good and well known teaches advanced students.) As much as she admired Agnes de Mille, the last thing Jamison wanted to do was take another class. Some friends talked her into it. It's a good thing. That was the night Jamison was "discovered."

De Mille immediately recognized Jamison's exceptional talent. She invited her to come to New York to be in a new

ballet called Four Marys that she was choreographing for the American Ballet Theatre. Needless to say, Jamison said yes.

COLLISION WITH DESTINY, PART TWO

Ironically, Jamison ran into Alvin Ailey after completely bombing out during an audition. In tears, she was so upset that she barely saw him. But, he had seen her—and the raw potential in her performance. He called her three days later to invite her to join his dance company. She became a member of the Alvin Ailey American Dance Theater in 1965. She toured the United States, Europe, Asia, South America, and Africa, danced with many of the world's greatest male dancers, and delighted audiences everywhere throughout the 15 years she danced with the company.

All this the result of a chance encounter in a hallway? Jamison prefers to think it was more like divine guidance. Those who have seen her dance would definitely agree.

BE READY WHEN SUCCESS COMES KNOCKING

In her autobiography, *Dancing Spirit* (New York: Doubleday, 1993), Jamison says:

> A lot of young people I meet do not know what they want to do with the rest of their lives, while it's getting later and they're under pressure to make a decision. It's for them not to worry, but to be well prepared, open, and educated. Learn as much as you can about everything. It's hard to tell young people to be patient, but that's what they need to be.

P.S.

Speaking of Jamison's autobiography, get it, read it, enjoy it, and learn some valuable lessons from someone who's made an incredible contribution to the world of dance.

Cosmetologist

SKILL SET

✔ ART

✔ BUSINESS

✔ TALKING

GO find a reputable stylist and try a daring new hairstyle.

READ fashion and hairstyle magazines to stay current on the latest trends.

TRY doing makeovers on your friends. Do hair, manicures and pedicures, and makeup.

WHAT IS A COSMETOLOGIST?

Cosmetologists work with individuals of all ages to keep them looking good. They routinely perform hair care procedures such as shampooing, styling, coloring, perming, and straightening. They can be most creative when they determine how to enhance each person's appearance with just the right style. Such creativity involves breaking out of a "cut of the month" mode and instead adapting the latest hairstyle trends into unique and attractive styles.

While hairstylist may be the first specialty that comes to mind, there are actually a number of additional specialties associated with cosmetology.

Estheticians specialize in skin care, body care, and makeup. While many work in beauty salons or spas, others work as makeup artists for television and movie studios or with plastic surgeons and dermatologists.

Electrologists specialize in removing unwanted hair from various parts of the body.

Manicurists specialize in hand and nail care. Manicures and pedicures are traditional services. As more women have discovered the convenience and appeal of various types of artificial nails, many salons and boutiques specialize exclusively in nail care.

Other possibilities include working as a photo stylist, a representative for a cosmetic company, a fashion consultant, or a cosmetology school instructor.

Cosmetology can also be an appealing option for those interested in owning their own businesses. In fact, owning or managing a salon is frequently part of the career progression for a successful cosmetologist.

In the United States, cosmetologists must become licensed before beginning to serve the public. Depending on the state, you can expect to spend between 1,000 hours (6 months) to 2,500 hours (15 months) in training. Cosmetology training includes classroom instruction in subjects such as hygiene and business practices as well as training in specific services such as facials and hair and scalp treatment. A good portion of the training involves practicing and actually performing the techniques learned in class.

Cosmetology training is often offered through high school vocational and technical training programs. You'll want to find out if this is an option in your school. However, before enrolling in any cosmetology training program, make sure that it has a good reputation. The early training you receive can make a big difference in determining who wants to hire you when you get out. Get the best, most reputable training you can find.

Actually obtaining a license involves providing proof of training, passing a written exam, and demonstrating various cosme-

tology services such as cutting, perming, and styling someone's hair. Before you even start thinking about licensing exams, you'll want to make sure that you pass these four tests.

- ☼ Attitude check. Are you friendly? Do you enjoy working with people? How well do you handle criticism?
- ☼ Artistic aptitude. Are you creative? Do you like to experiment with different styles and fashions? Are you willing to try new things?
- ☼ Care quotient. All aspects of cosmetology involve serving people in a very personal way. Do you care enough about people to do your very best work day after day, client after client? Is it important to you to boost others' self-esteem by improving their appearance?
- ☼ Physical fitness. Are you in good health? Do you have the stamina to work on your feet every day in a physically demanding profession?

In the United States, beauty salons serve at least 2 million people every day. That means there are plenty of employment opportunities for those with talent and perseverance.

☞ TRY IT OUT

BEAUTY BY THE BOOK
Start keeping a scrapbook of hairstyle and makeup ideas. You'll find tons of this kind of information (with some great photographs) in any fashion magazine. Clip pictures and add your own notes.

CUT OR DARE
Whatever you do, don't start experimenting with scissors on your hair or anyone else's. Instead, fine-tune your technique on hair that is not attached to a human head. Garage sales and thrift stores can be inexpensive sources of wigs. Feel free to practice styling and cutting to your heart's content without worrying about making mistakes.

LATHER UP

If you think you might like to become a cosmetologist but aren't sure, spend some time hanging out at a few good salons. You might even arrange to help out by shampooing clients or cleaning up for a favorite stylist in exchange for watching him or her work his or her beauty magic.

✔ CHECK IT OUT

🖱 ON THE WEB
VIRTUAL BEAUTY

You can learn a lot about this profession without leaving home by tapping into Internet resources. First stop is the Beauty Net at http://www.beautynet.com. Here you'll find a virtual hair studio, skin-care suite, makeup counter, tanning room, and nail salon. You'll also find out about new products and the latest trends.

Another fun stop is the Beauty Tech at http://www. beautytech.com. This site offers links to beauty industry sites and information about hair and nails. Unravel the secrets of hair at http://library.thinkquest.org/26829/i_e.htm.

📚 AT THE LIBRARY

Get a group of friends together who share an interest in fashion and style. Ask each person to style his or her hair and to dress in his or her usual way. Take a "before" picture of each individual.

Experiment with new makeup, clothes, and hairstyles (no cutting, please). When you're satisfied with the new look, take an "after" picture of each person. Take the film to a one-hour photo-developing company and enjoy seeing the results of your efforts.

For inspiration before you attempt the makeovers, take a look at the following books:

Jordan, Jim. *Hair Styling Tips and Tricks for Girls*. Middleton, Wis.: American Girl Library, 2000.

Kauchak, Therese. *Real Beauty: 101 Ways to Feel Good About You*. Middleton, Wis.: American Girl, 2004.

Naylor, Caroline. *Beauty Trix for Cool Chix: Easy-to-Make Lotions, Potions, and Spells to Bring Out a Beautiful You*. New York: Watson Guptill, 2003.

Wallace, Mary, and Jessica Wallace. *The Girl's Spa Book: 20 Dreamy Ways to Relax and Feel Great*. Richmond Hill, Ont.: Maple Tree Press, 2004.

Warrick, Leanne. *Hair Trix for Cool Chix: The Real Girl's Guide to Great Hair*. New York: Watson Guptill, 2004.

Williams, Julie. *Skin and Nails: Care Tips for Girls*. Middleton, Wis: American Girl, 2000.

While you're waiting for your nails to dry, join fictional detective Nancy Drew on a caper in:

Keene, Carolyn. *Secret of the Spa (Nancy Drew All New Girl Detective)*. New York: Aladdin, 2005.

🗣 WITH THE EXPERTS

American Association of Cosmetology Schools
15825 North 71st Street, Suite 100
Scottsdale, AZ 85254-2187
http://www.beautyschools.org

National Cosmetology Association
401 North Michigan Avenue, 22nd Floor
Chicago, IL 60611-4255
https://www.ncacares.org

Professional Beauty Association
15825 North 71st Street, Suite 100
Scottsdale, AZ 85254-2187
http://www.abbies.org

GET ACQUAINTED

Laurent Dufourg, Hairstylist

CAREER PATH

CHILDHOOD ASPIRATION: To become a musician.

FIRST JOB: Shampoo boy at a salon in France.

CURRENT JOB: Owner of Privé, an upscale beauty salon favored by many Hollywood celebrities.

MARCHING TO A DIFFERENT DRUM

Whenever she couldn't find a babysitter, Laurent Dufourg's mother took her son to the beauty salon on Saturdays. Now known on a professional basis simply as Laurent, he has fond childhood memories of days spent hanging out and trying to help by sweeping the floors while his mother tended to her hair and beauty regimen.

When it came time to pursue a career, however, his first choice was to become a musician. As a teen growing up in Biarritz, France, he played in a band and had big hopes for a music career. When he was 16 and needed money to buy new drums, his friend found him a summer job as a shampoo boy at a local hair salon.

Laurent discovered that he really liked the creative aspect of styling and knew this was the type of work he could enjoy. So, he arranged to apprentice with the world famous Claude Maxime in Paris and spent three years working and learning in the salon's various departments. (France doesn't require beauty school licensing like the United States does. Instead, stylists are trained through apprenticeships with established salons.)

A few years later, a client asked him to go to Spain as her personal stylist. This assignment took him to a beautiful resort on the Costa del Sol. Discovering a serious lack of beauty care services there, he opened two salons of his own. Both were a big hit with the wealthy and famous people who frequented the resort.

When his family relocated to Los Angeles, Laurent became partners with the famous hairstylist Jose Eber. They opened and operated five highly successful salons. In 1995, Laurent sold his share in this business to open Privé, his own salon on Melrose Place. The business has expanded to include branches in New York and Las Vegas and an exclusive line of hair-care products called Laurent D.

ALL IN A DAY'S WORK

On any given day, Laurent might be booked solid with appointments with glamorous stars such as Gwyneth Paltrow, Sharon Stone, Alicia Silverstone, or Lisa Kudrow. Or he might fly out to London for the day to do Uma Thurman's hair for a photo shoot. Another day might find him busy meeting with movie producers, directors, the wardrobe consultant, and makeup artists to discuss just the right look for Elisabeth Shue's new movie. A hard day's work might be capped off by escorting a client such as Paula Abdul to a movie premiere or award ceremony.

Not all jobs in cosmetology are this glamorous, but it's not hard to believe that Dufourg really loves his work. He says it's fun to be part of all the excitement in Hollywood.

WHEN LESS IS MORE

Two traits have helped Dufourg earn his reputation as a world-class hairstylist. First, Dufourg's clients know that they can trust him to be diplomatic and discreet. His elegant European sense of style and his genuine concern for his clients serve him well in a profession so reliant on forming good relationships with people.

Second, it is Dufourg's trademark to cut and style hair in ways that perfectly fit each client's looks, personality,

and lifestyle. His goal is to keep things as simple as possible because he understands that people are far too busy to have complicated hairstyles.

Together, these traits keep an impressive list of clients happy and coming back for more.

THE SECRET TO HIS SUCCESS

Dufourg says a stylist can never stop learning. He keeps up with the latest trends and techniques by attending fashion shows and special training classes, reading magazines, and always being on the lookout for good ideas he can reinvent for a particular client.

Development Director

SKILL SET

✔ ART

✔ TALKING

✔ WRITING

WHAT IS A DEVELOPMENT DIRECTOR?

Development directors, or fund-raisers, find creative ways to raise money for charitable causes. If the arts is your passion but not necessarily your forte (for example, you love ballet, but you can't dance), a career in development can put you right in the thick of things.

The best fund-raisers raise money for charitable causes that they really believe in. It's a lot easier to ask someone for money if you believe that it changes lives or somehow makes the world a better place.

Most fund-raising is quite sophisticated. Successful fund-raising usually involves researching likely sources of support (wealthy individuals, foundations, corporations, etc.), writing compelling grant proposals, organizing appealing programs, and maintaining long-term relationships with potential donors.

Most fund-raisers are employed by a specific organization—a performing arts group, museum, or social service program. Some fund-raisers specialize in planning special events such as charity balls, telethons, or walkathons. Others work for consulting firms that specialize in managing major fund-raising campaigns for projects such as building a multimillion dollar performing arts center.

You can also work for an organization that makes donations. Foundations and many large corporations actually employ people to give money away to carefully selected worthy causes. At foundations these people are usually called grant officers or administrators, and at corporations they are usually part of the public relations or community development staff.

Helping the arts (or another cause) flourish, giving away someone else's money—these are some careers to consider if you enjoy "doing good." What a way to make a living!

☞ TRY IT OUT

JOIN THE CLUB!

Arts organizations everywhere would welcome your interest in volunteering. Even though you don't get paid, carefully chosen volunteer projects will give you two important benefits. First, you get a chance to lend a hand to a cause you believe in or enjoy. Second, it gives you experience and contacts for future reference.

Be prepared: most volunteering involves varying degrees of behind-the-scenes dirty work. Play it smart; give every task your best effort. Such sacrifices have a way of paying big dividends down the road.

JUST DO IT!

You've probably been fund-raising since you were in kindergarten but didn't realize it. All those candy sales, car washes, and silent auctions are ways that schools, clubs, churches, and other groups make money for special projects (such as buying computers, playground equipment, and band uniforms). Get some more practice as a fund-raiser for your school. Hustle, think up new ways to sell; it's all for a great cause.

Always remember these rules of thumb, however: Get your parents' permission, let them know where you'll be and for how long, stick around familiar territory, and always move around in groups—never work alone.

THE MILLION-DOLLAR QUESTION: WHAT WORKS?

Add up all the fund-raisers that a typical school sponsors each year—with sports teams, clubs, the band, etc.—and you're likely to have the makings of some great market research.

First, ask around and find out what groups did to earn money. Second, make a chart. Put the name of the group in one column, the type of fund-raiser in another, and the purpose of the fund-raiser in a third. Next, ask the person in charge of the group for details about how much they earned. Get as specific as possible. For instance, ask how many items were sold, at what cost, and for what profit. Also find out how many people helped and, if possible, find out about how much time each person spent on the project. Add this information to your chart.

Finally, compare the results of each fund-raiser to determine which was most successful. Take it a step further by trying to figure out why. This ability to analyze situations carefully is a critical skill for a professional development officer.

COMPUTER BUCKS

As with so many other professions, the Internet is making work much easier for the professional fund-raiser. On the Net you can discover news about federal grants, research about corporate donors, and all kinds of pertinent data and statistics.

The first spot to visit is the National Endowment of the Arts home page at http://www.arts.endow.gov/. Here you will find a gold mine of information about funding for arts organizations. From this spot, you can also find your way to arts-related organizations all over the country. Just click on the Arts Resources option.

Other sites to browse include the Smithsonian Museum (http://www.si.edu), the Metropolitan Museum of Art (http://www.metmuseum.org), and any local arts and culture sites you can find with the help of your favorite Internet search engine. Also, run a word search on the specific areas of the arts that you have a special interest in—opera, ballet, performing arts, etc.

✔ CHECK IT OUT

🖱 ON THE WEB
NONPROFITS TO THE RESCUE

Arts organizations aren't the only charitable (or nonprofit) organizations supported through the efforts of development directors.When disaster strikes anywhere in the world, development directors everywhere spring into action, raising money to help make things right again. Learn about how some of the most prominent disaster relief organizations are making the world a better place at the following Web sites:

- ☼ America's Second Harvest at http://www.secondharvest.org
- ☼ Humane Society at http://www.hsus.org
- ☼ International Red Cross at http://www.redcross.org
- ☼ Salvation Army at http://www.salvationarmy.org
- ☼ Save the Children at http://savethechildren.org

📚 AT THE LIBRARY
CHARITABLE CASE STUDIES

Find out more about some of the world's most important philanthropic organizations in the following books:

Grant, R.G. *Amnesty International*. New York: Chelsea House, 2005.

Hastings, Terry. *Peace Corps*. New York: Chelsea House, 2005.

Parry, Ann. *Doctors Without Borders*. New York: Chelsea House, 2005.

———. *Red Cross*. New York: Chelsea House, 2005.

———. *Save the Children*. New York: Chelsea House, 2005.

WITH THE EXPERTS

Alliance of Nonprofit Management
1889 L Street NW, 6th Floor
Washington, DC 20036-3801
http://www.allianceonline.org

Association of Fundraising Professionals
1101 King Street, Suite 700
Alexandria, VA 22314-2944
http://www.nsfre.org

The Foundation Center
79 Fifth Avenue
New York, NY 10003-3034
http://fdncenter.org

American Association of Museums
1575 Eye Street NW, Suite 400
Washington, DC 20005-1105
http://www.aam-us.org

American Symphony Orchestra League
33 West 60th Street, 5th Floor
New York, NY 10023-7905
http://www.symphony.org

National Assembly of Local Arts Agencies
1000 Vermont Avenue NW
Washington, DC 20005-4903
http://www.nasaa-arts.org

GET ACQUAINTED

Richard Steckel, Fund-Raising Consultant

CAREER PATH

CHILDHOOD AJPIRATION: To play with the Brooklyn Dodgers—like most of the boys in his New York neighborhood.

FIRJT JOB: Involved a little bit of everything—collecting glass soda bottles for two-cent refund, delivering newspapers and groceries, busboy, waiter.

CURRENT JOB: Author, consultant, seminar leader.

IF HE ONLY KNEW THEN . . .

When Richard Steckel looks back on his life, he notes several "magic moments" that forged his destiny. One occurred when he was just eight years old. He was so intrigued by a movie he watched about a shipwreck off the coast of Australia that he instinctively knew, whatever he did with his life, it had to involve international travel. So far, his work has taken him to 70 countries that include Canada, Australia, Argentina, Chile, and Nigeria.

A second important event occurred when he was in eighth grade. He had a social studies teacher who was adored by all the girls. He liked the idea of being liked, so he decided to pursue a teaching degree in college.

Another life-altering experience occurred when he was a teenager. He saved up his own money from odd jobs to help reconstruct a church in Chile after an earthquake. This empowering experience made him realize that it was possible for one person to make a difference in others' lives.

COLORADO, HERE WE COME

Steckel's work in development took on a new dimension when he became director of the struggling Denver Children's Museum. It was there that he revolutionized the way nonprofit organizations support themselves. He developed marketing strategies that linked kid-friendly projects with corporate sponsors, staged some phenomenally successful special events (Trick or Treat Street is still a Denver favorite), and put some fun into fund-raising. You can read about these escapades in Steckel's book *Filthy Rich and Other Nonprofit Fantasies: Changing the Way Nonprofits Do Business in the 1990's* (Berkeley, Calif.: Ten Speed Press, 1991).

PRACTICING WHAT HE PREACHES

Now Steckel not only travels the world helping nonprofit organizations help others, but he has also established a nonprofit organization of his own. The organization is called the Milestones Project and its goal is to inspire 100 million people to reduce prejudice, intolerance, and hatred. To achieve this, Steckel, in collaboration with a team his wife, Michele, creates and disseminates wonderful resources that celebrate our common "milestone" experiences that make us part of the human race. For instance, everyone has a birthday, everyone loses a first tooth, and everyone has chores. For their book *The Milestone Project* (Berkeley, Calif.: Tricycle Press, 2004), the Steckels traveled around the world taking photographs of children experiencing these milestone moments.

BE TRUE TO YOURSELF

Steckel's career reflects an interesting journey of involvement in the things that matter most to him. He grew up in the 1960s and found himself smack in the middle of the civil rights and anti–Vietnam War movements. Thus, his values were forged during a time of social upheaval.

As a result, he found that a core value for him was that his work advance more choices for people—in education, work, and overall quality of life. This value has been part of every career decision he's made.

IT'S A GREAT REASON TO GET UP IN THE MORNING

Development is one of those careers in which the more you care about the cause you are working for, the more successful you will be. Choose an area in which you'd gladly spend your free time, be it sports, opera, or charity. By approaching it this way, work moves beyond being just the "hired gun" to raise money; it lets you live and breathe the issue.

READY OR NOT!

If you feel strongly about something, even if it doesn't have a name, don't give up on it. The world may not be ready for your ideas yet. Hang in there, read, talk to people, and make choices that are best for you.

STECKEL'S "DEC" THEORY

Determination, Enthusiasm, and Curiosity are always valued. Keep these traits handy, and they'll take you places.

Fashion Designer

SHORTCUTS

GO join the "teen fashion board" of a local department store.

READ about current fashion trends in fashion magazines and catalogs from favorite stores.

TRY making a list of fashions that are "in" and "out" at your school this year.

SKILL SET

✔ ART

✔ BUSINESS

✔ TALKING

WHAT IS A FASHION DESIGNER?

The clothes you are wearing right now say something about your attitude. They might be saying things like

- ☼ "I'm cool."
- ☼ "I couldn't care less."
- ☼ "I'm preppy."
- ☼ "Don't mess with me."

Whether you realize it or not, your fashion statements are the result of someone else's hard work. Fashion designers keep up on the latest trends and attitudes to design clothes that meet the needs of everyone from the newest baby to the oldest grandparent.

It takes a lot of people-watching and window-shopping to stay one step ahead of the next fashion craze. Fashion designers have to know what's hot and what's not. Since they are always working ahead toward the next season's fashions, they have to make careful distinctions (sometimes known as educated guesses) between last season's hits and next season's sensations.

Designers may work on anywhere between 50 and 150 designs for each season. Their work starts with detailed sketches of each design (either drawn by hand or by computer). The designer then makes pattern pieces for the garment (sometimes this is done by a pattern-maker or assistant). The pattern is used to cut carefully selected fabric to size in order to make a sample garment.

Samples are shown to buyers, and either the orders start rolling in or the designer goes back to the drawing board to incorporate suggested changes. The buying process often takes place at seasonal fashion shows.

There is an edge of glamor attached to this creative profession. However, fashion designers are just as likely to be employed designing the latest looks in underwear and children's play clothes as they are in the high-profile world of Paris couture. No matter what you're designing though, a career in fashion can be a creative way to put your artistic flair to good use.

Training for a career in fashion design usually involves attending an art school that specializes in fashion design or a more traditional college or vocational/technical school that offers a major in fashion design or textiles and clothing. A typical program will cover topics such as fashion development, consumer demand, fashion research and analysis, fabric production, apparel design development, and manufacturing processes. Of course, there will also be plenty of opportunity to hone your design skills.

You can start preparing yourself for this profession now by taking as many courses as possible in art (especially painting, sketching, sculpture, and screen printing), sewing, and computer-aided design (CAD). Psychology courses can also be useful in gaining a better understanding of human nature.

The fashion design industry is huge; in New York alone it does an estimated $14 billion in business per year. In a business this big, there's always room for fresh, new talent. Perhaps you'll be the creative force behind the next big fashion trend.

 **TRY IT OUT**

TRACK THE TRENDS
It's out with the old, in with the new. If you dream of becoming a designer, start training your eye for fashion now. Start keeping a fashion journal with sketches and clippings of the hottest looks for each season—spring and fall.

Date each entry and make sure to update the journal every year. By the time you graduate from high school, you are bound to have quite an interesting collection of fashion's hits and misses.

SKETCHES TO WEAR
The ultimate test of whether or not you should become a fashion designer is whether or not you can design fashions. Sketch ideas of clothes you'd like to wear. Use current fashions as a starting point, but remember, don't copy—create! Compile your best sketches in a scrapbook.

Then you might want to enlist the help of an accomplished seamstress (ask around among your friends or relatives) to make a sample of one of your designs. Better yet, learn to sew yourself (this is a must if you intend to go on to fashion school).

For ideas and inspiration, visit the Fashion Planet Web site at http://www.fashion-planet.com. At this address you'll find the latest fashion news and gossip as well as updates on the latest trends and emerging looks.

For tips on how to make fashion sketches, read:

———————————

Muehlenhardt, Amy Bailey. *Drawing and Learning about Fashion.* Minneapolis: Picture Window Books, 2005.

———————————

 CHECK IT OUT

🖱 ON THE WEB

CYBERFASHION

As part of the Smithsonian Institution, New York's Cooper-Hewitt National Design Museum is home to an extensive collection of drawings, prints, decorative arts, textiles, and wall coverings. Wander through some of the world's best design work by linking up with the museum's Web site at http://www.si.edu/ndm. Also, visit the Fashion Institute of Technology Museum Web site at http://www.fitnyc.edu/museum.

SNEAK A PEEK AT THE LATEST FASHIONS

Fashion shows are an integral part of the fashion scene. Attend as many as you can. Department stores can be good sources of seasonal trunk shows.

New York City, Chicago, Dallas, Atlanta, and Los Angeles are among the fashion manufacturing hot spots in the United States. Other cities specialize in specific areas of fashion. In Denver, it's skiwear, in Boston it's bridal gowns and accessories, and in Miami it's swimwear. Check your local phone book to locate manufacturers near you. The fashion pages of the local newspaper will also be a helpful source of information about fashion-related events in your area. Of course, if you get the chance to attend the big shows in New York,

Milan, or Paris, don't hesitate. In the meantime, an online experience may have to do. Go behind the scenes with these fashion-savvy Web sites:

- ☼ Explore the online home of *Vogue* and *W* at http://www.style.com/fashionshows.
- ☼ Find photographs taken at the most exclusive international fashion shows at http://www.fashionshowroom.com.
- ☼ Check out the latest in teen fashion news at http://teenfashion.about.com.
- ☼ Tune in to fashion TV at http://www.ftv.com/home/default.asp.
- ☼ Meet some aspiring fashion designers at http://www.kidkountry.com/fashion/fashion.php.

AT THE LIBRARY

MORE THAN MEETS THE EYE

The world of fashion offers an interesting array of career options. Some require extensive training and experience; others require a good dose of pluck and plenty of hard work. All require fashion sense and confidence in your abilities to make a contribution in a competitive field. Careers related to fashion design include manufacturer's representative, model, window display designer, fashion writer or photographer, accessory designer, fabric stylist, and costume designer.

You may find the following books particularly useful in helping sort out fashionable career options.

Kent, Jacqueline. *Business Builders in Fashion.* Minneapolis: Oliver Press, 2003.

Maze, Stephanie. *I Want to Be a Fashion Designer.* New York: Harcourt, 2000.

Pleasant Company. *Help Wanted: Fashion Designer.* Middleton, Wis.: Pleasant Company, 1999.

Wallner, Rosemary. *Fashion Designer Career Exploration.* Mankato, Minn: Capstone Press, 2000.

Vogt, Peter. *Career Opportunities in the Fashion Industry.* New York: Facts On File, 2002.

Also, update your fashion sense with these fashion encyclopedias:

Ware, L. Rowland. *Eyewitness: Costume.* New York: DK Publishing, 2000.

Wolf, Alex. *The Twentieth Century: History of Fashion and Costume.* New York: Facts On File, 2005.

🗣️ WITH THE EXPERTS

American Apparel and Footwear Association
1601 North Kent Street, Suite 1200
Arlington, VA 22209-2127
http://www.americanapparel.org

Council of Fashion Designers of America
1412 Broadway, Suite 2006
New York, NY 10018-9228
http://www.fgi.org

Fashion Group International
8 West 40th Street, 7th Floor
New York, NY 10018-3902
http://www.fgi.org

International Association of Clothing Designers and Executives
124 West 93rd Street, Suite 3E
New York, NY 10025-7536
http://www.iacde.com

GET ACQUAINTED

June Beckstead, Fashion Designer

CAREER PATH

CHILDHOOD ASPIRATION:
To be a veterinarian. She had 24 hamsters at one time to prove it!

FIRST JOB: Selling clothes at a retail shop.

CURRENT JOB: Vice president of KMart design group

WHEN ONE PLUS ONE EQUALS FASHION

June Beckstead had always enjoyed art as a child. She briefly lost touch with her artistic talent in high school. However, she discovered another creative area that she really enjoyed when she started working in a clothing store.

When she graduated from high school, Beckstead was indecisive about her future. During a heart-to-heart talk, her father encouraged her to think about what she liked to do. She liked art; she liked clothes. Put the two together, and you've got a career in fashion.

To this day, Beckstead is grateful that her father had the insight to guide her toward her talent and interests.

OFF AND RUNNING

Beckstead earned a degree in fashion design from the Fashion Institute of Technology and started her career by freelancing for a small award-winning company. Starting in a small company proved invaluable because it gave Beckstead a chance to learn about every aspect of the business: the design room, the pattern room, the showroom, and the public relations side of things.

The only downside to this experience was that she couldn't walk into a store and find the clothes. Beckstead solved that problem by accepting a position as vice president of women's product design for the Gap, Inc. During her 15 years with the company she and a team of designers were responsible for designing seasonal lines of women's clothing that typically included 100 sweaters, 100 knit items, and 100 woven pieces (including all the different colors and patterns for each piece).

A WELL-DRESSED CAREER

Before accepting her current position, Beckstead spent two years painting and teaching fashion design at Parsons School of Design in New York. There she worked primarily with graduating seniors and especially enjoyed the opportunity to educate prospective designers on what it takes to succeed in the field of fashion design.

In 2003, Beckstead was offered a position at Kmart which at the time was in its early stages of a turnaround. There she heads up the women's, girls', and baby design effort and works with a great design team who have worked with both high-end designers and mass-market retailers. Their job is to bring good design at great value to the customer. In other words, they work hard to make the inexpensive look expensive—just like the real thing. Her team works hard to get the best fabric, color, print, and silhouette for each garment—a process that Beckstead finds particularly challenging and rewarding.

A VOICE OF EXPERIENCE

A strong portfolio is a must for getting anywhere in the fashion industry. Beckstead has these tips for making sure your portfolio is noticed:

☀ Include at least 15 illustrations—well-mounted and professionally displayed—of designs using either male or female figures.

☼ Make sure the designs "tell a story" with a beginning, middle, and end. The story should involve coordinating fabric and seasonal themes.

☼ Show an understanding of the manufacturing process by including flat sketches of the front and back of each design, illustrating even the tiniest details such as seams and buttons.

☼ Demonstrate where you found the inspiration for your designs by putting together a "mood board" with tearsheets from magazines, postcards, fabric swatches, and any other sources of ideas.

In the end, advices Beckstead, it's your portfolio and your persistence that will sell your skill as a fashion designer.

Floral Designer

SHORTCUTS

GO to your local farmer's market and get acquainted with the types of flowers grown in your home state.

READ gardening magazines—supermarkets, bookstores, and newsstands have many fun choices. Pick one that appeals to you.

TRY arranging a centerpiece for the dinner table. Either buy a few fresh flowers and some greens from the florist or go outside and see what kind of creative ingredients you can come up with.

WHAT IS A FLORAL DESIGNER?

Floral designers play a part in people's best days and worst days. Their work helps people celebrate the high points in life and offers comfort during the low points of life. Weddings, birthdays, holidays, and funerals are just a few of the occasions when flowers are used as an expression of celebration or condolence. If you've ever been the recipient of a surprise bouquet, you know how effective flowers can be.

If doing your own thing creatively appeals to you, it may be worth your while to find out more about this profession. Whether it's with fresh, dried, or silk flowers, floral designers (or florists) use flowers to create moods, communicate important messages, and enliven the everyday lives of others. If you want your artistic ability to be noticed and appreciated, being a florist is a great way to do it. A beautiful flower arrangement is guaranteed to be the center of attention in any room.

Floral designers often work for retail stores that specialize in producing and delivering flower arrangements. Sometimes they also own the stores and must incorporate keen business management skills into their daily responsibilities. Others specialize in special events, such as weddings and big parties, and work directly for bridal shops, catering companies, or even funeral homes. Freelance designers succeed by developing good working relationships with wedding and event planners.

Some flower aficionados actually grow flowers in nurseries or on flower farms. Others sell flowers wholesale to retail shops, acting as liaison, or middleman, between the growers and the sellers. It is becoming increasingly common for florists to work in supermarkets, serving as designers, buyers, and shop managers. This arrangement can offer a satisfying mix of variety and experience. Another related profession involves the care and feeding of plant life in public places and/or offices.

The profession obviously demands a thorough knowledge of flowers coupled with a sense of color and design. For those who operate their own shops or nurseries, strong business skills are a must too.

There are no formal training requirements for floral designers. The nature of the work lends itself to on-the-job training or an apprenticeship (a formal on-site training situation where you learn from an experienced designer). For those who prefer a more structured training program, flower arranging courses can be found through some flower shops or continuing education programs.

Those designers who hope to one day own their own shops may want to consider pursuing a special certification through a community college or commercial floral design school. These programs typically offer courses in horticulture, marketing, and business management, as well as more intensive training in floral design.

Floral design is an appealing option for those looking for both a means of artistic expression and a means of helping others. The work is fairly evenly paced, although things can get hectic around certain holidays. Of course, spending your workday surrounded by beautiful flowers can also be a definite plus.

 TRY IT OUT

A PICTURE IS WORTH A THOUSAND WORDS
Look through some old magazines and cut out pictures of all the different flower arrangements you can find. Paste each picture to a separate sheet of paper. Use the following questions (recommended by the prestigious Rittner's Floral School) to critique each arrangement from an artist's point of view.

- What shape is the design?
- How many flowers are in the design?
- What kinds of flowers are in the design?
- What occasion is the design for?
- Where do you think a design like this would be best placed?
- What colors are in the piece?
- How are the colors placed?
- Is the floral design formal or informal? Traditional or contemporary? Seasonal?
- Does the floral design evoke a mood? If so, how?
- How do you feel about the floral art? Do you like it? Why?

BOTANICAL CRASH COURSE

While you still have those magazines and scissors handy, use them to find pictures of specific types of flowers. Paste each picture on a separate page in a notebook. Use a library book on botany or flowers to identify each variety. Label each picture with both its common and scientific name. Use the margin to jot down notes about other facts you discover about each flower (for example, special care instructions, native habitat, or traditions associated with the flower). Get started at the Society of American Florists' online flower library at http://www.aboutflowers.com/fpvar/fresh.html.

Just for fun, you may also want to learn the language of flowers. Flowers don't talk in actual words, but they certainly communicate very specific messages. Nothing says love quite like a rose. So, if a carnation represents joy, which flower represents hope? Use the following Web sites to find out: http://www.thegardener.btinternet.co.uk/flowerlanguage.html and http://www.pioneerthinking.com/flowerlanguage.html.

After you've learned all you can about as many flowers as you can, make a visit to a flower shop and get better acquainted with these newfound friends. Notice the smell, the texture, and the leaves. Memorize every detail. All this advance training will go a long way to impress a potential employer someday!

HOW DOES YOUR GARDEN GROW?

Growing your own garden can be a wonderful way to cultivate a relationship with flowers. Whether you start with a flower pot or an entire plot of land, get some seeds and start planting!

✔ CHECK IT OUT

🖱 ON THE WEB

ONLINE FLORIST SCHOOL

Continue your self-guided floral design education by learning the basics of arranging flowers. The following Web sites will help get you started:

 Rittner's School of Floral Design at http://www. floralschool.com

- ☀ Society of American Florist's Web site at http:// www.aboutflowers.com/floral_b2.html
- ☀ Flower of the month club at http://www. flowermonthclub.com/bouquetarrangementtips. htm
- ☀ Arranging tips at the HGTV Web site at http:// www.hgtv.com/hgtv/dc_floral_arrangements

A WEB SITE BOUQUET

For a garden variety of flower-related Web sites, visit some of the following:

- ☀ Celebrating Wildflowers at http://www.nps.gov/ plants/color
- ☀ Official State Flowers at http://www.50states.com/ flower.htm
- ☀ Kid's Valley Garden at http://www.raw-connections. com/garden
- ☀ My First Garden at http://www.urbanext.uiuc. edu/firstgarden
- ☀ Science of Gardening at http://www.exploratorium. edu/gardening
- ☀ If Plants Could Talk at http://www.ifplantscouldtalk. rutgers.edu
- ☀ Kid's Zone at the Junior Master Gardner Web site at http://jmgkids.us

 AT THE LIBRARY

BLOOMING BOOKS

For extra fun, take one of the following books to your favorite outdoor park and enjoy learning more about flowers.

Albian, Molly. *Life Cycle of a Flower*. New York: Crabtree, 2004.
Appelt, Kathi. *Miss Lady Bird's Flowers: How a First Lady Changed America*. New York: Harper Collins, 2005.

Bial, Raymond. *A Handbook of Dirt*. New York: Walker Books for Young Readers, 2000.

Burnie, David. *Plant: Google e-Guide*. New York: DK Publishing, 2006.

Eagan, Rachel. *The Biography of Sugar*. New York: Crabtree, 2005.

Farndon, John. *Flowering Plants: In Touch with Nature*. Farmington Hills, Mich.: Blackbirch Press, 2004.

Ray, Deborah Kogan. *The Flower Hunter: William Bartram, America's First Naturalist*. New York: Farrar, Straus and Giroux, 2004.

Roger, Ellen. *The Biography of Spices*. New York: Crabtree, 2005.

Spilsbury, Louise. *How Do Plants Grow?* Portsmouth, N.H.: Heinemann, 2005.

————. *Why Do Plants Have Flowers?* Portsmouth, N.H.: Heinemann, 2005.

Walker, Niki. *The Biography of Cotton*. New York: Crabtree, 2005.

Zronik, John. *The Biography of Rice*. New York: Crabtree, 2005.

The next two books are beautiful, detailed books written for an adult audience.

Hillier, Malcom, and Stephen Hayward. *Flowers: The Book of Floral Design*. New York: DK Publishing, 2000.

Pryke, Paula, and Kevin Summers. *Flowers: The Complete Book of Floral Design*. New York: Rizzoli, 2004.

🗣️ WITH THE EXPERTS

American Institute of Floral Designers
720 Light Street
Baltimore, MD 21230-3850
http://www.aifd.org

Association of Specialty Cut Flower Growers
MPO Box 268
17 1/2 West College Street
Oberlin, OH 44704-3850
http://www.ascfg.org

Flower Market Association
120 West 28th Street
New York, NY 10001-6109
http://www.fmanyc.org

Society of American Florists
1601 Duke Street
Alexandria, VA 22314-3406
http://www.safnow.org

GET ACQUAINTED

Ariella Chezar, Floral Designer

CAREER PATH

CHILDHOOD ASPIRATION: To be an actress or opera singer.

FIRST JOB: Babysitting, mowing lawns, and busing tables.

CURRENT POSITION: Floral and event designer.

CAREER PATH

Ariella Chezar is not your garden variety floral designer. With two gardening books to her credit, a slew of feature stories in national magazines like *Oprah*, *Martha Stewart Weddings*, *Victoria*, *Elegant Bride*, and *Town and Country*, she has carved out quite a name for herself with distinctive floral designs that grace weddings and parties on both coasts.

The funny thing is that Chezar didn't originally set out to become a floral designer. She was actually pursuing a degree in classical music at the University of Massachusetts when everything changed. Having already reached the conclusion that she didn't "need" a career as an actress or opera singer badly enough to make the total commitment necessary to pursue one; she was open to new ideas. Instant inspiration came one day when she visited the floral studio of a family friend who, at the time, was surrounded by an incredible array of extraordinary flowers in preparation for a wedding. Chezar said that the idea of working with the medium of beautiful flowers provided an immediate connection that "this is what I want to do."

ONE OF A KIND TRAINING

It wasn't long after this fateful day that Chezar stopped taking classes at the university and started an apprenticeship in the Berkshires with her friend, Pamela Hardcastle. Chezar says that instead of going to an official "floristry" school, she purposely chose a more nontraditional approach to learning floral design. She sought out mentors with unique styles and learned to cultivate her own artistic sensibilities.

Of course, Chezar says other factors along the way nurtured her creative bent. For one thing, her mother was a Dutch artist and their home was full of her paintings, their closets were full of clothes she made for her family, and their backyard was full of beautiful gardens. Chezar also credits years spent in an alternative school that fostered art and creativity.

According to Chezar's Web site, she describes her unique style in the following way: "Some artists use flowers creatively to have an edge, to be different. I look to the flower growing in its natural state as my inspiration. Rather than work against the inherent grace of each flower by packing them too closely together or forcing them to be uniform, I allow them breathing space to arch and move as they might. The possibility for drama comes in through the combinations of texture and color, which, whether contrasting or layered tone upon tone are always consciously thought out and never garish."

A FLOURISHING CAREER MOVE

Her first foray into the floral business involved selling wreaths to New York flower shops and to shoppers along the streets of SOHO and Greenwich Village.

She left New York for the West Coast in 1998 where she launched what has become a very successful business by doing the flowers for a friend's wedding for free. It was a big event held in a nice hotel. The hotel event coordinator was so impressed by Chezar's work that she started sending prospective brides to Chezar. Things, Chezar says, just snowballed from there.

Now she focuses her work on major weddings and parties held all over the country. She also continues to create wonderful books like *Weddings in Full Color* (San Francisco: Chronicle Books, 2002) and *Flowers for the Table: Arrangements and Bouquets for All Seasons* (San Francisco: Chronicle Books, 2002).

WORDS TO GROW ON

There are two things Chezar thinks aspiring floral designers should know. One is that floral design is really hard work. Playing with flowers is only one aspect of the business. She says that about 90 percent of arranging flowers involves preparing them—whether it's selecting them, dethorning them, trimming them, or any number of hands-on tasks.

The second thing she suggests is that floral designers consider rounding out their educational training by taking courses in botany or art history, actually growing flowers in a garden, and getting exposed to art on many levels. These outlets provide inspiration and help budding designers cultivate the instincts and ideas that will make their work stand out as truly unique.

To find out more about Chezar's work, visit her Web site at http://www.ariellaflowers.com.

Graphic Designer

SHORTCUTS

GO join up with your school's yearbook or newspaper staff for some firsthand experience.

READ all the magazines and look at all the greeting cards that you can. They provide a great introduction to contemporary graphic design.

TRY designing a poster to publicize a school or community event.

WHAT IS A GRAPHIC DESIGNER?

Imagine that you receive two equally important pieces of mail. It is obvious that one was typed up quickly (the misspelled words are a dead giveaway) and printed out on a cheap inkjet printer. Some of the words are smudged, and to make it even harder to read, it looks like a bad copy of a pretty bad original.

In contrast, the other piece is printed on thick, glossy paper. It even feels good. Bright colors and exciting visuals jump out, practically shouting, "Read me!" The piece includes headlines, bullets, and other graphic elements that make it easy to scan, guaranteeing that you'll notice the important details.

Which one of these two documents would you read first? It's entirely possible (and quite likely) that you'd throw away the first one before even looking at it. It doesn't demand your attention like the second one does. Even though the first piece contains information that is every bit as important as the second one, it would likely be completely ignored.

Why is that? We live in a visual age, and we require color, style, and pizzazz to get and keep our attention.

This is very good news for graphic designers, because their job is to provide the look for all kinds of materials, making sure they get seen, read, and remembered. Good graphic design can make a lasting impact. If you don't believe it, just take the following little quiz. See if you can think of the company behind the following elements:

- 💡 Golden arches? (Answer: McDonalds)
- 💡 Multicolored apple? (Answer: Apple computers)
- 💡 Big swoosh mark? (Answer: Nike athletic shoes)

These are examples of corporate logos. They help provide visual identity for big and small corporations. The goal is that when we see the logo, we instantly associate it with the company and its products (of course, the real goal is that we eventually buy something from the company, but that's another story).

Logos are just one way that graphic designers use a keen sense of artistic style combined with a working knowledge of various elements of design to create visually memorable materials. These same techniques are applied to book jackets, magazine and newspaper layouts, restaurant menus, and even weekly grocery store advertisements.

While natural artistic ability is helpful, an eye for design is a skill that can be learned, and in a variety of settings. Excellent training programs can be found at every level from trade school to graduate school. You may even find that your high school offers computer graphics classes.

Before you decide how much schooling you'll need, you'll have to decide what kind of specialty you want to pursue. A few graphic arts specialties to consider include:

animator	fashion illustrator	science illustrator
art director	medical illustrator	textile designer
cartoonist	multimedia designer	video designer
desktop publisher	publication designer	web designer

In addition to offering an appealing variety of specialties, graphic design is a profession that offers a number of employment options. It probably won't surprise you to learn that many graphic designers work for marketing and advertising companies. However, they also work in publishing houses, manufacturing firms, department stores, and government agencies. Computers and other high-tech equipment have made self-employment or freelancing a lucrative option for many an experienced and well-connected graphic designer.

If you want to use your artistic talent to beautify the things people read for business, education, or entertainment, graphic arts is a field to consider.

 **TRY IT OUT**

WEB REPORT CARDS

All kinds of companies use graphic design to get the attention of the people they want to buy their products. Since you, as a kid, are the intended audience of the companies in the following list, check out their online look and see if they got it right. First, though, use a blank sheet of paper to make a chart with space for the names of at least five companies. Include four columns ("A" for excellent, "B" for pretty good, "C" for not too bad, "D" for kind of blah, "F" for complete dud) so that you can grade each company on how well it does in these four areas: Fun look, Easy use, Interesting information, Exciting games and activities. These Web sites provide links to lots of other sites that the "experts" say are kid-friendly. Visit them and see if you agree.

☼ Run around the block? Visit Verb Now at http:/www.verbnow.com.

☼ Grab a chocolate bar? Visit Hershey's at http://www. hersheys.com/fun

☼ Visit a museum? Visit the Exploritorium at http:// www.exploritorium.edu.

☼ Buy a doll? Visit the American Girl store at http:// store.americangirl.com

☼ Rev up your engine? Visit the Hotwheels Web site at http://www.hotwheels.com

☼ Watch TV? Visit the Nickelodeon at http://www.nick. com

LEGENDARY LOGOS

A good logo provides instant identification for corporations or products. Brush up on some logo basics at the following Web sites:

☼ Read the Wikipedia entry on logos at http:// en.wikipedia.org/wiki/Corporate_logo.

☼ Find out what makes a great logo at http://www. code-interactive.com/thinker/a112.html.

☼ See a library of corporate logos at http://www. allthelogos.com.

Then use what you learn about logos to design one for your school, sport team, favorite club, or other important part of your life.

JUDGING A BOOK BY ITS COVER

Think fast! What's your favorite book? Try to visualize the theme of the story. Now grab a piece of paper and a pen, pencil, or markers and sketch out a cover that captures the essence of the story. Use another sheet (or sheets) of paper to refine your idea until you have the makings of a best-selling cover design.

Go to the library, a bookstore, your own bookshelf (or wherever you keep your personal collection of books), or online to Amazon (http://www.amazon.com) and find a copy of the book. Compare your cover to the publisher's.

THE GOOD, THE BAD, AND THE AWFUL

Eventually, you'll need your own portfolio as a graphic designer. For now, you can learn a lot from the work of other graphic designers. You'll need to go only as far as your family's mailbox or stack of magazines for ideas.

Paste a variety of different kinds of written communications—everything from advertisements to greeting cards to a club newsletter—on large pieces of paper. Use a marker to list the best and worst features of each design. Take note of things like color, the use of different types of letters (called fonts), pictures, the kind of paper. What catches your eye? Is it a pleasure to look at or is it cluttered and confusing?

Keep your collection in a notebook or folder, organized in order from your favorite design to your not-so-favorite ones. To get an idea of the details graphic designers think are important in designing good (or not so good) materials go to the Web Pages That Suck Web site at http://www.web-pagesthasuck.com. After you've seen the worst, take a look at the best at the Webby Awards Web site at http://www.webbyawards.com.

 CHECK IT OUT

🖱 ON THE WEB

GRAPHIC DESIGN ONLINE

Tips, ideas, and tutorials are all to be found at the following Web sites:

- ☼ Find ideas for students at the American Institute of Graphic Arts Web sites at http://www.aiga.org/content.cfm/students.
- ☼ Learn how to create your own Web site at http://www.webgenies.co.uk/indexnoflash.htm.
- ☼ Find out how to make and use great graphics at http://www.kidsturncentral.com/topics/computers/htgraphics.htm.

📚 AT THE LIBRARY

READ ALL ABOUT IT

The following lineup of books provides insight into various aspects of graphic design.

Bentley, Nancy, and Donna Guthrie. *The Young Journalist's Book: How to Write and Produce Your Own Newspaper.* Minneapolis: Millbrook Press, 2001.

Diehn, Gwen. *Making Books That Fly, Fold, Wrap, Pop Up, Twist and Turn.* New York: Sterling, 1999.

Fox, Gabrielle. *The Essential Guide to Making Handmade Books.* Cincinnati: NorthLight Books, 2000.

Marcus, Leonard. *Side by Side: Five Favorite Picture Book Teams Go To Work.* New York: Walker Books for Young Readers, 2001.

———. *Ways of Telling: Fourteen Interviews With Masters of the Art of the Picture Book.* New York: Dutton Juvenile, 2003.

Pedersen, Ted. *Make Your Own Web Page for Kids.* New York: Scholastic, 1998.

Selfridge, Benjamin. *A Kid's Guide to Creating Web Pages.* Chicago: Zephyr Press, 2004.

🗣 WITH THE EXPERTS

American Institute of Graphic
  Arts
164 Fifth Avenue
New York, NY 10010-5901
http://www.aiga.org

Art Director's Club
106 West 29th Street
New York, NY 10001-5301
http//www.adcglobal.org

Graphic Artists Guild
90 John Street, Suite 403
New York, NY 10038-3202
http://www.gag.org

Society of Publication Designers
17 East 47th Street, 6th Floor
New York, NY 10017-1920
http://www.spd.org

GET ACQUAINTED

Gary Pettit, Graphic Designer

CAREER PATH

CHILDHOOD ASPIRATION: To be a musician.

FIRST JOB: Acting in summer stock theater from age four.

CURRENT JOB: Visual design director at Starwest Productions, a family-owned corporation.

IT ALL STARTED WITH THE THREE LITTLE PIGS

Gary Pettit has always been good at art. He recalls a first-grade drawing assignment that the teacher hung on the wall. Even then, his drawing of the three little pigs showed promise.

The funny thing is that he spent a good deal of his youth immersed in art and various forms of the arts (his whole family was musically inclined and had the acting bug). Yet Pettit never dreamed it would result in a profession, until one thing led to another, people started paying him for his work, and a great business was (almost accidentally) launched.

PETTIT'S FIFTEEN MINUTES OF FAME

The three Pettit brothers—Steve, Phil, and Gary—sang together as a trio and appeared on a number of stages throughout the Rocky Mountain region. They also made some radio commercials. Their claim to fame, however, was producing a record album to help raise money for crippled children. It didn't seem like such a big deal then, but Pettit recognizes the experience as one of those rare and wonderful opportunities in life.

A FAMILY AFFAIR

Today, Pettit, with his two brothers and their parents, runs a thriving business that utilizes everyone's best skills. Phil is the computer whiz, Steve is the creative director, and Gary rounds things off with his artistic expertise. Dad is a semiretired mechanical engineer but is always available for advice and ideas. Mom is the office manager and keeps everyone in line.

A LITTLE OF THIS, A LITTLE OF THAT

Pettit applies his creative genius to a variety of projects from developing logos and point-of-sale materials for an up-and-coming beverage company to developing promotional campaigns to generate excitement about (and ticket sales for) new movies for a national chain of theaters. Ditto for a national commercial realty company. He also spends a good deal of time on sports marketing materials, poster design, video clips, traveling exhibitions, and much more.

TOP-OF-THE-LINE PRODUCTIONS

Whether he works in film, video, multi-image, display materials, or print, Pettit has built a solid reputation for producing some good stuff. So good, in fact, that his work has been honored with awards from national organizations such as the Public Relations Society of America, the Institute of Real Estate Management, the International Association of Business Communicators, the Association for Multi-Image, and the Chicago International Film Festival.

A PART OF THE COMMUNITY

The Pettit family has lived in Colorado for a couple generations. Metro Denver is home, and life there has been good to them. That's just one of the reasons why they donate so much of their time and talent to support causes that they believe in. Whether it's putting together an incredibly scary haunted house to earn money for a favorite charity or designing a newsletter to get the word out about a shelter for victims of abuse, Pettit follows a family tradition of making a contribution

to his community. In addition to their efforts close to home, the Pettits also work with an international foundation and have helped raise more than 50 million dollars for children's charities all over the world.

DREAM WITH A NEW DIRECTION

For years, the Pettit brothers talked about developing their own theme park. They put together lots of great ideas and all sorts of plans and ideas and even got close to making a deal that would get things rolling. Over time their ideas have evolved and their common dream has changed in some interesting ways. They are currently designing a new office facility that will make going to work feel like going to a theme park.

Industrial Designer

SKILL SET

✔ ART

✔ MATH

✔ SCIENCE

WHAT IS AN INDUSTRIAL DESIGNER?

"Design is the way something looks and how it works. It's art. It's technology. It's an object, or group of objects. It's a plan, a sketch, a drawing. Something decorative, something functional. A pattern, a model, an invention. It's also a process: to think, plan, conceive, form, create, make, build, envision. Design is work. And play. A part of everyone's life. A measure of the quality of life."

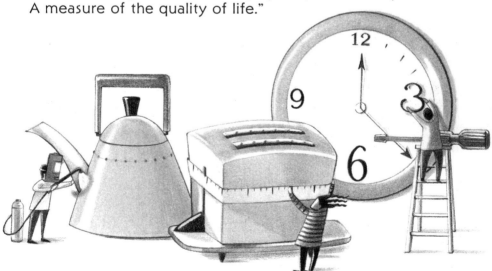

That's how a brochure about the National Design Museum sums up the design process. This museum houses some 30,000 three-dimensional applied arts and industrial design artifacts, from ancient times to the present.

The museum's official definition of industrial design is "the professional service of creating and developing concepts and specifications that optimize the function, value and appearance of products and systems for the mutual benefit of both user and manufacturer." In other words, it is the design of products manufactured by industrial processes.

The creative ideas of an industrial designer are behind some of your favorite everyday things: DVD and DVD players, laptop computers, cellular phones, microwave ovens, and plasma TVs, among other things. They all went through an intensive design process before you found them at the store. The desk and chair you use at school, disposable razors, and bicycle helmets—are all the result of an innovative industrial designer.

An industrial designer is part artist, part engineer, part inventor. Add a touch of the philosopher and a bit of business executive, and you'll have the perfect mix for an effective industrial designer. The industrial designer uses technology to solve real-world problems. He or she relies on customer research to design products that people need and want to buy.

According to the Industrial Designers Society of America (IDSA), industrial designers must know how to work with their heads as well as their hands. They must learn to see solutions where others see problems. They must know something about everything, as well as a lot about building things and making things happen.

Industrial designers are playing an increasingly important role in developing products that either take the market by storm or become long-running mainstays. Products such as the Apple iPod, Gillette's Sensor razor, and Reebok's Pump sneaker are examples of such hot sellers.

Industrial designers are just as likely to start their education at an art college or school of design as they are to start at a major university. A good industrial design training program is similar to an engineering program, with courses in mathematics, physics, and economics. The program should progressively introduce opportunities to apply one's growing knowledge to projects—making drawings, models, full-scale mock-ups, and eventually simulated finished projects. Internships and on-the-job training are particularly useful in this field.

So much in our world is affected by the design process. Everything from automobiles to zippers can use creative design to become more efficient, more environmentally friendly, and more cost-effective. Some products out there may be waiting for your creative input!

 TRY IT OUT

TIME TO INVENT
Use the information you find at http://inventors.about.com/od/timelines to create a timeline of the world's greatest inventions. Record your findings on a big piece of poster board (jazzed up with photos and colorful markers, of course) or use your computer to create a cool flowchart.

INVENT A FUTURE
Hey, have you heard? It's up to you (and your generation) to save the world. Everyone is counting your ideas, your innovations, your solutions to humankind's most perplexing problems to save the day, so you better get started now. Make a list of the nagging problems you encounter every day (heavy backpacks, for instance). Now think of ways technology could be used to improve or solve the situation. Come up with as many ideas as you can. Then pick your best idea and describe it in detail. What would it look like? How would it work?

Make your ideas official by using them to enter the Exploravision contest. This national contest is sponsored by Toshiba and the National Science Teachers Association to encourage young people to combine their imaginations with

their knowledge of science and technology to explore visions for the future. For information, visit http://www.exploravision. com/2005/index.htm.

 CHECK IT OUT

ON THE WEB

AND THE WINNER IS . . .

The Industrial Designers Society of America presents annual industrial design awards in the areas of business and industrial products, consumer products, design explora- tion, environmental design, furniture, packaging and design, transportation, and medical and scientific design. For some award-winning design inspiration, take a virtual a virtual stroll through the IDSA design galleries at http://www.idsa. org/galleries.

While you're at the Web site, download a copy of their "What is ID?" brochure at http://www.idsa.org/webmodules/ articles/articlefiles/what_is_id_brochure.pdf.

VIRTUAL IDEAS

Underneath every industrial designer is an inventor at heart. Find fascinating resources about inventors and their inven- tions at these Web sites:

- Explore Invention at http//invention.smithsonian.org
- How Stuff Works Express at http://www.express. howstuffworks.com
- Kids Invent! at http://www.kidsinvent.com
- National Geographic's Inventions at http://www. nationalgeographic.com/features/96/inventions
- National Inventors Hall of Fame at http://www. invent.org
- Zoom Inventors and Inventions at http://www. enchantedlearning.com/inventors

AT THE LIBRARY

INNOVATION AND INSPIRATION

Following are books sure to inspire some inventive ideas:

Bridgman, Roger. *1000 Inventions and Discoveries.* New York: DK Publishing, 2006.

Flatow, Ira. *They All Laughed: From Lightbulbs to Lasers.* New York: Harper Collins, 1999.

Jones, Charlotte. *Mistakes That Worked: 40 Familiar Inventions and How They Came to Be.* New York: Random House, 1999.

Thimmesh, Catherine. *Girls Think of Everything: Stories of Ingenious Inventions by Women.* New York: Houghton Mifflin, 2000.

Tomecek, Stephen. *What a Great Idea! Inventions That Changed the World.* New York: Scholastic, 2003.

Wulffson, Don. *The Kid Who Invented the Popsicle and Other Surprising Stories about Inventions.* New York: Dutton, 2001.

WITH THE EXPERTS

Corporate Design Foundation
20 Park Plaza, Suite 400
Boston, MA 02116-4303
http://www.cdf.org

Industrial Designers Society of America
45195 Business Court, Suite 250
Dulles, VA 20166-6717
http://www.idsa.org

Institute of Industrial Engineering
3577 Parkway Lane, Suite 200
Norcross, GA 30092-2827
http://www.iienet.org

GET ACQUAINTED

Anthony Grieder,
Industrial Designer

CAREER PATH

CHILDHOOD ASPIRATION: To become an architect.

FIRST JOB: Shipping clerk in a roll bar factory.

CURRENT JOB: President and owner of Alloy Design Inc. (http://alloydesign.us).

THE CLUES WERE THERE ALL ALONG

As a child, Anthony Grieder spent his spare time building intricate towns and buildings for little toy animals. Things got so elaborate that his family eventually had to set aside an entire room in the house for him to pursue this hobby.

As is so often the case, this childhood passion provided the groundwork for his ultimate career as an industrial designer. Now instead of dreaming up suitable habitats for rubber toys, he applies the same kind of careful, logical thinking to dreaming up new products for clients.

THE BEST DECISION HE'S EVER MADE

After deciding there wasn't much money to be made as a professional trombone player, Grieder pursued his childhood ambition of becoming an architect. He earned a bachelor's degree in environmental design and then spent the summer working for a distant relative's architectural firm in South Africa.

The only problem was that Grieder found the work boring. He felt himself separated from the creative process by tons of details and layers of architects with lots more experience than he had.

In need of a new plan, he decided to pursue a master's degree in product design. He says it's the best decision he's ever made. Now, instead of spending laborious hours on little details, he has seen some of his great ideas come to be a reality.

His first job on his new path as a designer involved helping design upscale shopping centers. Everything from the furniture and lighting to each of the storefronts was customized to make for a unique shopping experience. He started out as low man on the project, so he spent a lot of time constructing models that represented each idea—shades of childhood past!

THE DOCTOR IS IN

In recent years, Grieder has specialized in designing medical equipment as well as products for the data storage industry. One of his products won an award of excellence from the Rocky Mountain Chapter of the IDSA. The product, an attachment to pulse oximeters, was designed to save hundreds of feet of cable wire. The result was a huge savings in money and resources.

Other products that Grieder has had a hand in designing include a breath alcohol tester for police departments, a pair of shin guards for ski racers, and a machine combining a stair-climber and a treadmill for health clubs.

IN HIS DREAMS

Underneath Grieder's calm exterior lives a digital artist. His dream project would involve exhibiting digital photo art in galleries around the world.

BEST ADVICE

According to Grieder there are a couple things a young person can do now to start preparing for a career in industrial design. One is to read about specialized products such as cars, computers, housewares, etc. That's a good way to learn about the business and to cultivate an area of specialization.

Another all-important tip: Get good grades in school! Work hard now, and there will be more opportunities for you later.

Above all, always be open to new ideas. You never know where they'll take you.

Interior Designer

WHAT IS AN INTERIOR DESIGNER?

What do you think about a traditional approach? Maybe a more contemporary look is more to your liking? How about making things a bit cozier with a French country touch? Should you use chintz or a nice moiré to cover the sofa? Roman shades or wood shutters for the window?

All these choices and details make interior design a challenging and exciting profession. According to group consensus of several professional associations, the official definition for an interior designer is one who is "qualified by education, experience, and examination to enhance the function and quality of interior spaces."

This is done "for the purpose of improving the quality of life, increasing productivity, and protecting the health, safety, and welfare of the public."

This means that interior designers decorate people's homes and public places. Some designers specialize in design for specific spaces, such as

- ☼ businesses, offices, and industrial workplaces
- ☼ restaurants, hotels, resorts, and spas
- ☼ hospitals and other medical facilities
- ☼ retail stores, malls, displays, or exhibits
- ☼ churches, synagogues, and other places of worship
- ☼ schools and college campuses
- ☼ museums and theaters
- ☼ government facilities—including everything from the local post office to the White House
- ☼ transportation—trains, ships, airplanes, submarines, and spaceships

Still other interior designers specialize in set design—for theater, television, and movies—or in lighting design. Teaching, illustration, product development, and historic preservation are other outlets for the creative interior designer.

No matter what kind of space is involved, the process usually begins by discussing options with the client. The designer must listen carefully and ask the right questions to get an idea of what the client hopes to achieve in the space. Next, the designer sketches or uses a computer to draw pictures of various ideas. The sketch includes the furniture, special built-in features in the room, fabrics, colors, and the overall theme. The designer must be very careful to draw all elements to scale, making sure that they accurately represent the space.

Once a concept is approved, the designer must work with manufacturers, builders, and other workers to find all the materials and products necessary to carry out the design. This is where knowing who's who and what's what comes in very handy. A successful interior designer is a carefully balanced mixture of super shopper, detective, and supervisor.

Sometimes items can be purchased directly from a manufacturer; other times they have to be built to very detailed specifications. In every case, the designer must know the best and most affordable source of securing every single item needed to complete the design plan.

The process requires attention to every detail, thorough knowledge of design concepts, great contacts with suppliers, and a vivid imagination for conjuring up all the possibilities.

Though not rigidly required, professional training is generally expected. Interior design schools and some art schools offer three-year certification programs. Many colleges and universities offer four-year bachelor's degree programs. Wherever the education is obtained, an aspiring interior designer can expect to take courses in art history, architectural drawing and drafting, fine arts, and furniture design. Other courses will cover topics such as lighting, electrical equipment, and communication and business skills.

Although it is not necessary to obtain a license, working toward professional accreditation can be an asset in this field. Accreditation involves meeting specific training and experience guidelines and passing a national examination administered by the National Council for Interior Design Qualification. Upon meeting these criteria, a designer becomes eligible for membership in participating professional associations.

Interior designers help keep the world beautiful. They add zest and charm and comfort to the places where people live, work, and play. Their work involves an exciting mix of artistic expression and people-pleasing skills. The work is both creative and demanding.

 **TRY IT OUT**

DREAM HOUSE PRIMER

Pick out a pretty photo album filled with plenty of pages for mounting pictures. Designate a page or two for each room you hope to have in your ultimate dream house. Be sure to leave space for each bedroom and bathroom.

Make it a habit to thumb through every magazine you come across looking for decorating ideas. When you find a picture of something you especially like, clip it and put it in the appropriate spot in your planning album. Feel free to add sketches of your own and notes describing the features that you like best.

✔ CHECK IT OUT

🖱 ON THE WEB
COLOR YOUR WORLD

In interior design, as in fashion, color plays a huge role. Take a look around your classroom and see if you can identify the season's most popular colors.Then go online and learn all you can about color and the role it plays in our everyday life.

- 💡 Talking about Color at http://www.thetech.org/exhibits_ events/online/color/attributes
- 💡 Color Theory for Kids at http://members.cox.net/ mrsparker2
- 💡 The Colour Experience at http://www. colour-experience.org

CYBER DECORATING

Interior decorating plays a starring role in a growing number of television shows. Check out the following Web sites for information and resources:

- 💡 HGTV at http://www.hgtv.com
- 💡 Martha Stewart at http://www.marthastewart.com
- 💡 Trading Spaces at http://tlc.discovery.com/fansites/ tradingspaces/tradingspaces.html
- 💡 Interior design from A to Z at http://www. digital-librarian.com/home_interior.html
- 💡 Careers in interior design at http://www.careersin interiordesign.com

 ## AT THE LIBRARY

SNOOZE IN STYLE

Looking for ways to make a personal statement in your personal space? Look no further than the following books to find ideas and inspiration for giving your room a makeover.

American Girl. *Room Crafts: Add Some Simple Style to Your Space.* Middleton, Wis.: American Girl, 2004.

Banner, Shawn. *Room for You! Find Your Style and Make Your Room Say You!* Middleton, Wisc: American Girl Library, 2001.

Creative Publishing International. *Bedrooms for Cool Kids.* Chanhassen, Minn.: Creative Publishing International, 2002.

Jennings, Lynette. *Have Fun With Your Room: 28 Cool Projects for Teens.* New York: Simon Pulse, 2001.

Montano, Mark. *Super Suite: The Ultimate Bedroom Makeover Guide for Girls.* New York: Universe, 2002.

Oxmoor House. *Creative Publishing International. The Big Book of Teen Rooms.* Des Moines, Iowa: Oxmoor House, 2001.

DECORATING BY THE BOOK

You'll find decorating books by the dozens at the local library. The 747 section includes books on all aspects of decorating—basic decorating techniques, furniture styles, fabric, glassware, etc.

Compare the styles of different designers and see if you find one that you particularly like. See if you can pick out a favorite color combination. While you're there look for books about some of the latest decorating trends such as feng shui, sustainable design, and universal design.

WITH THE EXPERTS

American Society of Interior Designers
608 Massachusetts Avenue NE
Washington, DC 20002-6006
http://www.asid.org

Environmental Design Research Association
PO Box 7146
Edmond, OK 73083-7146
http://www.edra.org

Foundation for Interior Design Education Research
146 Monroe Center NW, Suite 1318
Grand Rapids, MI 49503-2833
http://www.fider.org

Interior Design Educators Council
7150 Winton Drive, Suite 30
Indianapolis, IN 46268-4399
http://www.idec.org

National Council for Interior Design Qualification
1200 18th Street NW, Suite 1001
Washington, DC 20036-2506
http://www.ncidq.org

GET ACQUAINTED

Kaki Hockersmith,
Interior Designer

CAREER PATH

CHILDHOOD ASPIRATION: To be an actress or writer.

FIRST JOB: Working in her dad's advertising agency.

CURRENT JOB: Runs her own interior design firm.

MAKING THE MOST OF EVERY OPPORTUNITY

Kaki Hockersmith never really intended to become an interior designer. She went to college, majoring in English and history and minoring in speech and art. Then she graduated, got married, and became a schoolteacher. She taught for a while, but when she was offered the chance to help produce an educational history series for the local public television affiliate, she jumped at it.

After that project was over, a long-time friend offered her a position as a designer for a chain of fashionable department stores. Always willing to keep her options open, Hockersmith accepted the position. Her job was to decorate the "vignettes" (those little rooms) in the furniture departments. She had to plan the color scheme and accessories, decide how to arrange the furniture, and make sure that each of the stores had everything they needed to put it together. In this job, she learned the ropes of interior design and discovered she had a natural talent for the work.

She eventually started her own decorating business in Little Rock, Arkansas. She says she learned as she went along and sometimes wished she had professional training in the field. She worked hard and paid some hard dues in the process.

However, it all paid off when she won the commission to redecorate the governor's mansion in Arkansas. The governor at the time was Bill Clinton. He and his family so liked the comfortable English country look that she gave the family quarters that when they moved to Washington, D.C., they asked Hockersmith to serve as their official decorator.

A HOUSE IS A HOUSE (OR IS IT?)

While it's pretty exciting to be asked to decorate the White House, Hockersmith found the process to be similar to any other project. Her basic plan stayed the same: Consider the client's needs, consider the client's preferences, and consider how the room is used. The finished room is deemed a success only when all three of these standards are met.

Of course, the White House offered some important, historic considerations as well. Not every house has first picking in a warehouse filled with 40,000 square feet of museum-quality art and antiques. And not every project involves hordes of reporters following your every move and other famous designers analyzing every element of the design. The pressure was high and so were the stakes.

Fortunately for Hockersmith, the finished results are widely considered a smashing success. Her clients, President and Mrs. Clinton, were very pleased with the new look, and with her newfound fame, her career suddenly took on a global feel. Clients from all over the world sought her out. Hockersmith, however, remains closely connected with the White House as a presidential appointee to the Committee for the Preservation of the White House, an honor that affords her the opportunity to work in historic preservation on a grand scale.

HOCKERSMITH WAS HERE

Hockersmith works very carefully to make sure that each project she completes accurately reflects the tastes of her clients. She hopes never to become so boring that a person could immediately identify something as the Hockersmith signature style. There is only one thing that consistently marks every project she works on, and that is her attention to detail. She puts a lot of attention and planning into creating looks that appear unplanned. Her goal in any space is to make it "real" and to create a sense that somebody actually lives there—a little organized clutter usually does the trick.

WHEN YOU WISH UPON A STAR

One of the biggest perks of having a father in the advertising business was that Hockersmith often got to act in the commercials he produced for clients. She fondly recalls one occasion when she choreographed her own little dance to accompany the song "When You Wish Upon a Star." She performed the dance on a local television show while her mother was in the hospital giving birth to Hockersmith's younger sister.

Years later, when she was in Washington, D.C., to decorate the White House, she was relaxing in a restaurant when someone started singing that song. The memory came flooding back, and she was delighted to realize that dreams really can come true.

Museum Curator

SHORTCUTS

GO visit every museum you can find.

READ up on any interesting subject until you become an "expert" in that area.

TRY starting a collection of your own— stamps, butterflies, coins—that you can pursue with a passion.

SKILL SET

✔ ART

✔ HISTORY

✔ TALKING

WHAT IS A MUSEUM CURATOR?

Rock 'n' roll music, sports, trains, history, cars, fashion, art—all of these industries and interests have museums dedicated solely to them. With about 5,000 museums in the United States, there's something for everyone.

Museums can be run by federal, state, and local governments, nonprofit organizations, colleges, universities, businesses, professional associations, or private citizens. No matter where you find them or what their specialties are, all museums have one thing in common—their need for a curator to put (and keep!) it all together.

Museum curators, sometimes called collections managers, are the experts who develop and oversee the collection of artifacts or other special objects that give the museum its identity. For instance, a curator in a rock 'n' roll museum works with music memorabilia. Depending on the type of museum that they work for, curators might specialize in various types of art, coins, minerals, clothing, maps, animals, plants, or historic sites.

The curator at a typical museum carries many responsibilities, and his or her work involves several stages. First a curator must find and acquire interesting and historically significant objects that fit with the overall purpose of the museum. This stage involves a good deal of research and may require some travel to find the right pieces.

Once an object is located, the curator must determine whether the price is reasonable and affordable. Again research

is an invaluable tool in this process, because the curator must be certain that the piece is authentic and must be fully aware of its worth in order to do a good job.

Several verbs describe the next stages of a curator's work. Once an object has been obtained—either through a donation or through a purchase—the curator must appraise, insure, analyze, describe, arrange, catalog, restore, preserve, exhibit, maintain, and store it. Some museums have very large staffs, and these duties are divided among them. The curator or another professional takes on the task of arranging the piece in museum exhibits so as to be enjoyed by the museum's visitors. The curator may also help develop various publications and resources to help educate others about the collection. Some curators also spend time actually teaching others about the exhibits.

Finally, curators must keep careful records about each of the items in their collections and go to great lengths to protect each item while it is on display and in storage.

A good education is key to securing a career as a curator. Most curators are highly skilled with advanced degrees. In some of the larger museums, it would be fruitless to apply for a position as a curator without a PhD. Fortunately, there are many ways to build your base of experience while learning your way to the top.

Many aspiring curators work at various positions within a museum before assuming the full responsibility of curator.

Other museum-related occupations include

administrator, who handles the business side of running a museum in matters such as personnel, budget, and building maintenance. A museum administrator is often in charge of making sure that all the various departments in a museum run smoothly.

archivist, who works with important historical documents, photographs, films, and other information sources. The archivist's job is to find them, organize them, keep records about their origins and whereabouts, and make them available to the people who might need them. Depending on what type of museum or library that an archivist works for, he or she might handle historical documents such as the Declaration of Independence, letters from famous people such as presidents or actors, or special records from important business meetings.

conservator, a highly trained specialist who examines, repairs, and restores art objects. A conservator must be knowledgeable in the science of chemicals and apply what he or she knows about the effects of pollution, the environment, and light on various types of art.

registrar, who acts as a legal guardian for a museum and is in charge of all the paperwork that must be kept about each artifact in the museum. The registrar keeps records that indicate where each piece is located, where it came from, how it is insured, how to care for it, and other vital information. A good registrar knows where to find every single piece in the museum's collection at all times—whether it's on display, on loan to another museum, or in storage.

Entry-level positions for people straight out of high school or college might include tour guide, exhibit educator, and gift shop clerk (with more training, gift shop manager or buyer could be an option as well).

There's a lot of work behind the exhibits you see at any museum. The job opportunities in museums are often quite competitive because they can be interesting and fulfilling. Thus, making the challenging quest for a career in this field is well worth the effort.

TRY IT OUT

PLAN YOUR OWN EXHIBIT

Talk to your school principal or religious leader about your interest in becoming a museum curator. Explain that you'd like the opportunity to test your skills and ask for help in putting together an exhibit about the history of your school or place of worship. Some of the things you might look for on the history of your school are old photographs of the building and its principals, teachers, and students; newspaper clippings about major events such as sports championships; old yearbooks; and maybe even an old sports or band uniform. Talk to as many people as you can about the early days. If your school is too new for this idea, try your church or temple.

Once you've gathered all your materials and received permission to display them, practice arranging them in different ways to get an interesting, visually attractive exhibit that will make sense to viewers. You'll want to write a description of each item and attach it so that viewers can fully understand its significance.

If you find it difficult to find actual artifacts to display, you might want to write a chronology of events from the beginning to the present. You can list these events on posters or in a special booklet.

MUSEUM ADVISOR

Visit a local museum—it doesn't matter what kind. Take a notebook and pencil with you, and plan on staying for a while. Gather the available written materials about the exhibit. Read them carefully to get a better idea of what the exhibit is all about. Then take a slow and observant tour of the exhibit. When you are finished, write down your overall impression of the exhibit. Was it interesting? Did it make sense? Could you move from one display to another relatively easily?

Now, take another walk through the exhibit. This time, list each displayed item in your notebook. Make a checklist and note the following:

- Is this object a good fit with the overall theme of the exhibit?

☯ Is the object displayed in an interesting and attractive way?

☯ Is the object described in an interesting and easy-to-understand way?

CHECK IT OUT

🖱 ON THE WEB

CLICK YOUR WAY TO THE WORLD'S MUSEUMS

You don't even have to leave home to tour some of the world's most impressive museums. Many are a step away, in living color, via the Internet. One exceptional Web site is called Internet ArtResources at http://artresources.com.

Make sure to stop by the kids sections of the following museums too:

☯ Children's Museum of Indianapolis at http://www.childrensmuseum.org/kids/kids.htm

☯ Exploratorium at http://www.exploratorium.edu

☯ Exploris at http://www.exploris.org/home.html

☯ Henry Ford Museum and Greenfield Village at http://www.hfmgv.org/explore/default.asp

☯ National Gallery of Art at http://www.nga.gov/kids/kids.htm

☯ Smithsonian Institute at http://www.smithsonian education.org/students

☯ Williamsburg at http://www.history.org/kids

 AT THE LIBRARY

ARMCHAIR MUSEUM TOUR

Can't get to a favorite museum? The following books provide a "next best thing to being there" experience with guided tours through some favorite museums and museum artifacts.

Bardham-Quallen, Sudipta. *The Louvre Building: Building World Landmarks.* Farmington Hills, Mich.: Blackbirch, 2005.

Barry, Sharon. *Official Guide to the Smithsonian National Museum of Natural History.* Wash., D.C.: Smithsonian Books, 2004.

Bay, Ann Phillips. *A Kid's Guide to the Smithsonian.* Wash., D.C.: Smithsonian Books, 1996.

Knapp, Ruthie, and Janice Lehmberg. *Off the Wall Museum Guides: American Art.* Worcester, Mass.: Davis, 1998.

————. *Off the Wall Museum Guides: Egyptian Art.* Worchester, Mass.: Davis Publications, 1998.

————. *Off the Wall Museum Guides: Greek and Roman Art.* Worcester, Mass.: Davis, 2001.

————. *Off the Wall Museum Guides: Impressionist Art.* Worchester, Mass.: Davis Publications, 1998.

————. *Off the Wall Museum Guides: Modern Art.* Worchester, Mass.: Davis Publications, 2001.

Poulakidas, Georgene. *The Guggenheim Museum Bilboa: Transforming a City.* Danbury, Conn.: Children's Press, 2004.

Richardson, Joy. *Inside the Museum: A Children's Guide to the Metropolitan Museum of Art.* New York: Henry N. Abrams, 1993.

Romanowsky, David. *Official Guide to the Smithsonian National Air and Space Museum.* Washington, D.C.: Smithsonian Books, 2002.

MORE MUSEUM ADVENTURES

Also, in the next-best-thing-to-being-there category is this smattering of fictional stories with plot lines that plop you down slap dab in the middle of some of very interesting museums.

Aver, Chris. *Hidden in Plain Sight.* Nashville, Tenn.: ZonderKids, 2005.

Brezina, Thomas. *Who Can Crack the Da Vinci Code? Museum of Adventures.* New York: Prestel, 2005.

————. *Who Can Save Vincent's Hidden Treasure.* New York: Prestel, 2005.

Koningsburg, E. L. *From the Mixedup Files of Mrs. Basil E. Frankweiler.* New York: Atheneum, 1967.

Scieszka, Jan. *Seen Art?* New York: Viking Children's, 2005.

WITH THE EXPERTS

American Association of Museums
1575 Eye Street NW, Suite 400
Washington, DC 20005-1105
http://www.aam-us.org

American Institute for Conservation of Historic and Artistic Works
1717 K Street NW, Suite 200
Washington, DC 20036-5346
http://www.aic.stanford.edu

Society of American Archivists
527 South Wells Street, 4th Floor
Chicago, IL 60607-3928
http://www.archivists.org

GET ACQUAINTED

Barbara Luck, Museum Curator

CAREER PATH

CHILDHOOD ASPIRATION: To use art, without being a teacher in the school system.

FIRST JOB: Museum registrar.

CURRENT JOB: Curator of paintings and drawings at the Colonial Williamsburg Foundation.

IT'S LIKE WORKING A GIGANTIC JIGSAW PUZZLE

Barbara Luck is responsible for the paintings and drawings—historical and contemporary—at Colonial Williamsburg. When she acquires a new piece of art, she does a careful study to track its history. Some of the questions she tries to answer are: Who

made it? Who used it? How was it used? And what did it mean to its owners? This research process can involve digging through volumes of old records and traveling to numerous places to talk to town historians and librarians. She looks for historic documentation as well as personal stories so that each piece comes alive with meaning to the people who visit the museum.

DOES IT PASS THE LUCK TEST?

Through the years, Luck has gained a keen sense of the type of artwork needed to round out the museum collection. Before acquiring something new, each piece must pass Luck's five-point test:

- Is this piece authentic?
- Does the museum need this piece?
- Can the museum afford this piece (or will someone donate it for free)?
- Can this piece be transported to the museum and displayed at the museum without being damaged?
- Is this piece unusual, important, historically significant, and aesthetically pleasing?

BIGGEST CHALLENGE

Luck finds challenge and great delight in making 18th-, 19th, and 20th-century materials relevant to today. She enjoys helping museum visitors of all ages relate what they see in the museum to their own lives.

ADVICE TO FUTURE MUSEUM CURATORS

Luck has these suggestions for aspiring curators:

1. Learn to respond visually to things around you.

2. Practice describing these things so that they interest and make sense to others.

3. Get a good education in a field that interests you, but be prepared to learn a lot about this profession on the job.

Photojournalist

SKILL SET

✔ **ADVENTURE**

✔ **ART**

✔ **WRITING**

GO snap a good photo at every opportunity.

READ *National Geographic* and *Life*, two magazines noted for exceptional photography.

TRY videotaping an event at school.

WHAT IS A PHOTOJOURNALIST?

The first man on the moon. The 9/11 attacks. Hurricane Katrina. Do any of those statements immediately evoke a vivid image in your mind? If so, it's probably because of a photojournalist.

Using both photography and journalism, photojournalists combine the two disciplines to tell compelling stories with pictures. They take pictures of newsworthy events, places, and people for newspapers, magazines, or television shows. They often specialize in a particular kind of photography such as news, sports, social issues, or documentaries. Some photojournalists focus on covering wars and international events.

Photojournalists can either be employed by a specific newspaper, news show, or magazine, or they can work on freelance assignments. Freelance means that they are self-employed. They work on special projects for a specific client, or they come up with their own ideas for photo essays and sell them to the appropriate media.

Photojournalists must be as familiar with current events and human nature as they are with photographic style and lighting techniques. Their job is to capture the mood and news of our world with a click of their camera shutter.

Related professions range from being a photographic supplier, working in the business of selling "tools" such as cameras, film, and processing equipment, to being a filmmaker, creating motion pictures for worldwide audiences. In between

these two extremes are many other opportunities. Commercial photographers work in areas that include advertising, public relations, and marketing. Studio photographers take pictures that mark important events in people's lives—baby's first picture, senior portraits, and the like. Photographers who specialize in the educational field may teach, produce audiovisual aids and training films, or provide appropriate pictures to illustrate textbooks.

There is quite a variety of training options for someone interested in a photography career. How much training you'll need depends on what you intend to do. For some jobs, high school photography courses provide all the training you need to get started. Others require a two- or four-year degree with a major in photography. A degree with some combination of photography and journalism would be useful for an aspiring photojournalist.

Learning from an expert through an apprenticeship is yet another option. If completed in a portrait or commercial studio, an apprenticeship could provide training in more than one aspect of photography, including film processing and lighting techniques.

Perhaps one of the most exciting aspects of photography is its potential to let you earn while you learn. For instance, if you've successfully completed high school photography training, you might find it possible to work in a studio while earning a college degree in photojournalism.

PHOTOGRAPHER ON THE LOOSE

Family reunions, school assemblies, nature hikes—someone interested in a photography career shouldn't be caught at events like these without a camera. Practice makes perfect when it comes to photography. Every time you develop a roll of film, you'll learn how to improve your technique.

Make sure you submit those especially good shots to your community or school newspaper. Every picture that gets published is another page for your photography portfolio. Future employers will be impressed that you had the courage and talent to get published as a teenager.

Put together a poster or scrapbook featuring some of your best shots.

MAKE A PHOTO SCRAPBOOK

You don't have to go any farther than your local supermarket or bookstore to find exceptional examples of photojournalism. Pick up copies of magazines such as *Life, National Geographic,* or *Sports Illustrated* and look for pictures that thrill and inspire. Clip these photos and paste them in a special notebook. Keep notes on where you found the photo, the name of the photographer, and what you like about the photograph. It won't be long before you can start adding your own photos to the scrapbook!

SMILE AND SAY CHEESE!

Where else but the Internet can you use state of the art technology (your computer) to find instructions for making an old-fashioned camera (a pinhole camera)? It's a fun project and can help you figure out how cameras do what they do. Here are a couple Web sites that provide instructions using different kinds of recycled materials:

⚲ Kodak Coffee Can Pinhole Camera at http://www. kodak.com/global/en/consumer/education/ lessonPlans/pinholeCamera/pinholeCanBox.shtml

- ☼ Oatmeal Box Pinhole Camera at http://users.rcn. com/stewoody
- ☼ Pringles Can Pinhole Camera at http://www. exploratorium.edu/science_explorer/pringles_ pinhole.html

✔ CHECK IT OUT

🖱 ON THE WEB

PEACE, LOVE, AND PHOTOGRAPHY

Fun, fame, and fortune are a couple reasons why photographers take pictures. But some photographers use their skills to change the world. For an example of the power of pictures, go online and read about the Milestones Project at http://www.milestonesproject.org/.This organization is using pictures to reduce prejudice and celebrate humanity.

You can also find examples of this organization's photography in the Richard and Michele Steckel's book *The Milestones Project* (Berkeley, Calif.: Tricycle Press, 2004).

GREAT PHOTOGRAPHY ONLINE

- ☼ Visit the American Museum of Photography at http://www.photography-museum.com.
- ☼ See a documentary of famous photographer Ansel Adams at http://www.pbs.org/wgbh/amex/ansel.
- ☼ Tour the Canon Camera Museum at http://www. canon.com/camera-museum.
- ☼ Go online to the Eastman Museum at http://www. eastmanhouse.org/inc/education/k-12.asp.
- ☼ Find photography project ideas at http://www. edutainingkids.com/articles/digitalcamerafun learning.html.
- ☼ Get ideas and information from the Kodak e-magazine at http://www.kodak.com/US/en/corp/magazine/ index.shtml.

 **AT THE LIBRARY**

A PICTURE IS WORTH A THOUSAND WORDS

The following books will shine some light on the basics of photography:

Bidner, Jenni. *The Kids' Guide to Digital Photography: How To Shoot, Save, Play With, and Print Your Digital Photos.* Asheville, N.C.: Lark, 2004.

Ewald, Wendy. *I Wanna Take Me a Picture.* Boston: Beacon Press, 2002.

Friedman, Debra. *Picture This: Fun Photography and Crafts.* Tonawanda, N.Y.: Kids Can Press, 2003.

Haslam, Andrew. *Photography: Make It Work.* Minnetonka, Minn.: Two Can Publishing, 2000.

Johnson, Neil. *Photography Guide for Children.* Washington, D.C.: National Geographic Children's, 2001.

Miotke, Jim. *Absolute Beginners Guide to Taking Great Photos.* New York: Three Rivers Press, 2002.

Weed, Paula. *Tricky Pix: Do It Yourself Trick Photography.* Palo Alto, Calif.: Klutz, 2001.

WITH THE EXPERTS

National Press Photographers Association
3200 Croasdaile Drive, Suite 306
Durham, NC 27705-2586
http://www.nppa.org

North American Nature Photography Association
10200 West 44th Avenue, Suite 304
Wheat Ridge, CO 80033-2837
http://www.nanpa.org

Professional Photographers of America
229 Peachtree Street NE, Suite 2200
Atlanta, GA 30303-1601
http://www.ppa.com

GET ACQUAINTED

Stephen Shames,
Freelance Photojournalist

CAREER PATH

CHILDHOOD ASPIRATION:
To be either a cowboy or a U.S.
senator.

FIRST JOB: Taking pictures of
the student protest movement
during the 1960s.

CURRENT JOB: Producing
documentary essays about social
issues.

Stephen Shames accidentally found his career as a photo-journalist when he was a history major at the University of California–Berkeley. He took a photography class at the student union, discovered that he was good at it, and concluded that it was more fun to earn his way through college taking pictures than washing dishes.

By the time he graduated, he had established himself as a credible photojournalist by covering the protest movement of the 1960s (ask your parents or teachers about groups such as the Black Panther Party, People's Park, and Angela Davis). When he left college, he worked as a freelance photojournalist for publications such as *Newsweek*, the *New York Times*, and *Time*.

PLACES TO LOOK FOR SHAMES' WORK

You can find Shames's work on the front page of a national newspaper, in national news magazines such as *Time* and *Newsweek*, on a television news program, in a school text-book, in an art museum exhibit, or in one of Shames's photo essay books—*Outside the Dream: Children in Poverty in America* (New York: Aperture, 1991) or *Pursuing the Dream:*

154

What Helps Children and Their Families Succeed (New York: Aperture, 1997). Also visit Shames's Web sites at http://www.stephenshames.com and http://www.outsidethedream.org.

THE PHOTOJOURNALIST AS AN ARTIST

Like other artists, professional photojournalists learn how to express their feelings through their art. Shames says that it takes a lifetime to move from taking pictures to producing art with a camera. Unlike other artists, photojournalists often have just a split second to create their art. Everything a photojournalist has learned about photography, people, and history has to come together in a flash to record the truly great moments in history.

BEYOND THE STARVING ARTIST MYTH

Freelance photojournalism is a competitive business. The people who treat it as a business are the ones who are most likely to make a good living at it.

One secret to success is making multiple sales from one project. For example, Shames once spent five months riding along in a squad car with the Houston homicide police. He took pictures of them as they answered calls, investigated cases, and interrogated suspects. Shames sold pictures from that project to a regional magazine, a national news magazine, a television news show, an encyclopedia publisher, and a textbook publisher. He used one of the photos in his own book on children in poverty. Some of the pictures were also featured in a six-page essay on domestic violence as part of a *Newsweek* story on the O.J. Simpson trial.

Shames is affiliated with Matrix, an international photo agency. They help him sell his photographs, including the homicide work.

SNAP TO IT

Photojournalists have to go to the news; they can't wait for news to come to them. This means keeping their bags packed and being ready to travel anywhere in the world on a moment's notice. Shames says that it's not unusual for a photojournalist to be on the road from 100 to 200 days a year.

YOU HEARD IT HERE FIRST

The industry is changing and will belong to those who can keep up with the change. Digital cameras and other high-tech equipment are redefining the industry. Some day soon photojournalists may be using small, high-tech camera phones when they cover stories in the field. One thing that will never change is that photojournalists will still be storytellers. No matter what the technology, the pictures will continue to be the key.

ADVICE TO FUTURE PHOTOJOURNALISTS

Think, stay ahead of the game, and learn to make your own opportunities.

MAKE AN ARTISTIC DETOUR!

Go ahead. Feel free to dismiss completely the notion of the starving artist. Once you realize that artistic career opportunities can include a full range of creative endeavors, you'll find about 1.3 million jobs per year in a $314 billion business.

That's big. So big, in fact, that some people estimate that one in three children will be employed in an arts-related occupation someday. That means many opportunities for the artistically inclined. If you don't believe it, just check out the following artistic ideas.

A WORLD OF ARTISTIC CAREERS

SHARE YOUR TALENT

Many who've been blessed with artistic talents of one kind or another have found great satisfaction in educating others. This route often provides the means of making art the focal point of a career while also providing a regular paycheck and opportunities for career advancement.

art education
curriculum writer
art historian
art librarian
art teacher
choir director
dance teacher

dance therapist
docent
museum educator
music libararian
musicologist
music therapist
piano teacher

school arts
coordinator
speech teacher
speech therapist
theater teacher
vocal music teacher

MAKE ART YOUR BUSINESS

Does it surprise you to discover that the business world is one of the best places to put your artistic talents to work? There are many ways to blend your artistic bent with the creative needs of business. A few ideas to consider include:

advertising artist
apparel engineer
art director
(advertising,
publishing, etc.)
arts marketer
automobile
designer
billboard artist
book illustrator
calligrapher
caricaturist
cartographer
clothing designer
color specialist
computer graphics
designer
display designer
draftsperson

equipment designer
exhibit designer
fabric designer
fashion cutter
floral designer
furniture designer
graphic designer
greeting card
illustrator
holographer
industrial designer
instrument manu-
facturer
interior designer
knitting designer
layout artist
leather goods
designer
lithographer

machinery designer
milliner
mold maker
music engraver
neon sign maker
newspaper illustrator
optical effects
engineer
ornament designer
package designer
paper maker
parade float designer
pattern designer
product designer
record cover
designer
retail buyer
shoe designer
software designer

sound effects technician
tattoo artist
textile designer

theme park designer
tile designer
toy designer
typographer

upholsterer
wallpaper designer
window designer
yarn dyer

NO MORE STARVING ARTISTS

If creating art in its purest and simplest form is what you want to do, here are some creative outlets to consider. Just remember, making it and selling it are two different things. Find a way to make it pay!

basket maker
bead maker
china painter/ designer
engraver
framer
glassblower
handicrafter
ice sculptor

instrument designer/ builder/repairer
jewelry designer
kinetic artist
knitter
lacemaker
muralist
needleworker
painter

photographer
potter
printmaker
sculptor
serigrapher
stained glass artist
tapestry artist
weaver
woodworker
xylographer

A POTPOURRI OF CREATIVE CAREER IDEAS

Put some creative thought into using your artistic talent in some unusual and even unexpected ways. Here are some ideas to get you thinking.

aerial photographer
aeronautical designer
anatomical diagrammer
archaeologist
architectural model builder
art appraiser
art conservator
artist's agent
arts and entertainment journalist
arts attorney
auctioneer

booking agent
contract specialist
copyright specialist
critic
environmental designer
facility planner
fund-raiser (development director)
gallery owner/ salesperson
glaze technologist
golf course designer
landscape architect

makeup artist
museum curator
music contractor
music editor
nightclub manager
photojournalist
piano tuner
police artist
program director (TV, radio, arts organizations, etc.)
ticketing agent
urban planner
writer

THE ROAR OF APPLAUSE

If you are an artist who can't resist the thrill of an encore performance, consider some of these career ideas that put you (or your work) in the spotlight.

accompanist
actor
announcer
art festival
  coordinator
artistic director
  (theater, film)
artist's agent
audio engineer
ballet dancer
band director
box office manager
casting director
choreographer
cinematographer
clown
comedian
composer
concert musician
concert promoter
concert singer
conductor
costume buyer

costume designer
cruise ship enter-
  tainment director
dancer
disc jockey
documentary
  producer
electric/acoustical
  engineer
keyboard technician
film editor
filmmaker
gaffer
instrumentalist
lyricist
magician
mime
motion picture
  animator
music publisher
news anchorperson
orchestrator
playwright

producer (TV, radio,
  theater, movies)
props designer
recording engineer
  and mixer
record producer
rigger
scene painter
screenwriter/
  scriptwriter
set designer
songwriter
sound engineer
stagehand
theater director
TV camera operator
videographer
vocalist
voice-over artist
wardrobe mistress/
  manager

KEEP IN MIND

Here are a couple of things to keep in mind as you continue to ponder the artistic possibilities.

Mix and Match Your Skills

Anything you can do in another field, you can do in the arts; for example, if you love math and the arts, think about becoming an accountant for an arts organization or museum. If you love all things technical and the arts, think about blending the two as a sound or lighting technician, a CD-ROM designer, or a

sound mixer. If arts and writing are your top two, think about a career as an arts reporter, a public relations specialist for an arts organization, or a development officer.

Whatever your unique blend of skills and interests may be, there's a creative way to mix and match them in an arts-related profession.

The Art of Show-and-Tell

Perhaps more than any other professional field, the art world relies on show-and-tell. Many of these professions are visually oriented. You can talk about painting a great picture, but you'll make more impact (and more commissions) if you can prove it.

That's why a portfolio is so important for artists of all kinds. A portfolio provides an orderly, visually attractive "résumé" of your work. It includes samples of your best work to showcase your personal style and achievements for prospective employers and clients. It's never too early to get into the portfolio habit. Start compiling your best work now.

DON'T STOP NOW!

GO FOR IT!

It's been a fast-paced trip so far. Take a break, regroup, and look at all the progress you've made.

1st Stop: Discover
You discovered some personal interests and natural abilities that you can start building a career around.

2nd Stop: Explore
You've explored an exciting array of career opportunities in this field. You're now aware that your career can involve a wide variety of options with many different educational and training paths to get you where you want to go.

At this point, you've found a couple careers that make you wonder "is this a good option for me?" Now it's time to put it all together and make an informed, intelligent choice. It's time to get a sense of what it might be like to actually have a job like the one(s) you're considering. In other words, it's time to move on to step three and do a little experimenting with success.

3rd Stop: Experiment

By the time you finish this section, you'll have reached one of three points in the career planning process.

1. **Green light!** You found it. No need to look any further. This is the career for you. (This may happen to a lucky few. Don't worry if it hasn't happened yet for you. This whole process is about exploring options, experimenting with ideas, and, eventually, making the best choice for you.)

2. **Yellow light!** Close, but not quite. You seem to be on the right path but you haven't nailed things down for sure. (This is where many people your age end up, and it's a good place to be. You've learned what it takes to really check things out. Hang in there. Your time will come.

3. **Red light!** Whoa! No doubt about it, this career just isn't for you. (Congratulations! Aren't you glad you found out now and not after you'd spent four years in college preparing for this career? Your next stop: Make a U-turn and start this process over with another career.)

Here's a sneak peek at what you'll be doing in the next section.

- ☼ First you'll pick a favorite career idea (or two or three).
- ☼ Second, you'll link up with a whole world of great information about that career on the Internet (it's easier than you think).
- ☼ Third, you'll snoop around the library to find answers to the top 10 things you've just got to know about your future career.
- ☼ Fourth, you'll either write a letter or use the Internet to request information from a professional organization associated with this career.
- ☼ Fifth, you'll chat on the phone to conduct a telephone interview.

After all that you'll (finally!) be ready to put it all together in your very own Career Ideas for Kids career profile (see page 175).

Hang on to your hats and get ready to make tracks!

#1 NARROW DOWN YOUR CHOICES

You've been introduced to quite a few art career ideas. You may also have some ideas of your own to add. Which ones appeal to you the most?

Write your top three choices in the spaces below. (Sorry if this is starting to sound like a broken record, but . . . if this book does not belong to you, write your responses on a separate sheet of paper.)

1. _____

2. _____

3. _____

#2 SURF THE NET

With the Internet, the new information superhighway, harging full steam ahead, you literally have a world of information at your fingertips. The Internet has something for everyone, and it's getting easier to access all the time. An increasing number of libraries and schools are offering access to the Internet on their computers, or you may have a computer at home.

A typical career search will land everything from the latest news on developments in the field and course notes from univer- sities to museum exhibits, interactive games, educational activities, and more. You just can't beat the timeliness or the variety of information available on the Web.

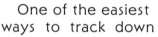

One of the easiest ways to track down this information is to use an Internet search engine, such as Yahoo! Simply type in the topic you are looking for, and in a matter of seconds, you'll have a list of options from around the world. For instance, if you are looking for information about companies that make candy, use the words "candy manufacturer" to start your search. It's fun to browse—you never know what you'll come up with.

Before you link up, keep in mind that many of these sites are geared toward professionals who are already working in a particular field. Some of the sites can get pretty technical. Just use the experience as a chance to nose around the field, hang out with the people who are tops in the field, and think about whether or not you'd like to be involved in a profes- sion like that.

Specific sites to look for are the following:

Professional associations. Find out about what's happening in the field, conferences, journals, and other helpful tidbits.

Schools that specialize in this area. Many include research tools, introductory courses, and all kinds of interesting information.

Government agencies. Quite a few are going high-tech with lots of helpful resources.

Web sites hosted by experts in the field (this seems to be a popular hobby among many professionals). These Web sites are often as entertaining as they are informative.

If you're not sure where to go, just start clicking around. Sites often link to other sites. You may want to jot down notes about favorite sites. Sometimes you can even print out information that isn't copyright-protected; try the print option and see what happens.

Be prepared: Surfing the Internet can be an addicting habit! There is so much awesome information. It's a fun way to focus on your future.

Write the addresses of the three best Web sites that you find during your search in the space below (or on a separate sheet of paper if this book does not belong to you).

1. _____

2. _____

3. _____

#3 SNOOP AT THE LIBRARY

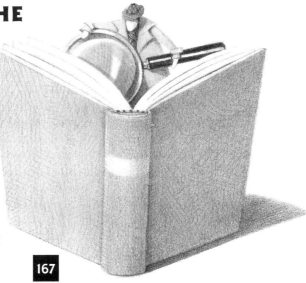

Take your list of favorite career ideas, a notebook, and a helpful adult with you to the library. When you get there, go to the reference section and ask the librarian to help you find books about careers. Most libraries will have at least one set

of career encyclopedias. Some of the larger libraries may also have career information on CD-ROM.

Gather all the information you can and use it to answer the following questions in your notebook about each of the careers on your list. Make sure to ask for help if you get stuck.

TOP 10 THINGS YOU NEED TO KNOW ABOUT YOUR CAREER

1. What is the purpose of this job?

_____

2. What kind of place is this type of work usually done in? For example, would I work mostly in a busy office, outdoors, or in a laboratory?

_____

3. What kind of time is required to do this job? For instance, is the job usually performed during regular daytime business hours or do people work various shifts around the clock?

_____

4. What kinds of tools are used to do this job?

_____

5. In what ways does this job involve working with other people?

_____

6. What kind of preparation does a person need to qualify for this job?

_____

7. What kinds of skills and abilities are needed to be successful in this type of work?

_____

8. What's a typical day on the job like?

_____

_____

9. How much money can I expect to earn as a beginner?

_____

10. What kind of classes do I need to take in high school to get ready for this type of work?

_____

#4 GET IN TOUCH WITH THE EXPERTS

One of the best places to find information about a particular career is to go to a professional organization devoted especially to that career. After all, these organizations are full of the best and the brightest professionals working in that particular field. Who could possibly know more about how the work gets done? There are more than 450,000 organizations in the United States, so there is bound to be an association related to just about any career you can possibly imagine.

There are a couple ways you can find these organizations:

1. Look at the "Check It Out—With the Experts" list following a career you found especially interesting in the Take A Trip! section of this book.

2. Go online and use your favorite search engine (such as http://www.google.com or http://yahoo.com) to find professional associations related to a career you are

interested in. You might use the name of the career plus the words "professional association" to start your search. You're likely to find lots of useful information online so keep looking until you hit pay dirt.

3. Go to the reference section of your public library and ask the librarian to help you find a specific type of association in a reference book called *Encyclopedia of Associations* (Farmington Hills, Mich." Thomson Gale) Or, if your library has access to it, the librarian may suggest using an online database called *Associations Unlimited* (Farmington Hills, Mich.: Thomson Gale).

Once you've tracked down a likely source of information, there are two ways to get in touch with a professional organization.

1. Send an e-mail.
   Most organizations include a "contact us" button on their Web sites. Sometimes this e-mail is directed to a webmaster or a customer service representative. An e-mail request might look something like this:

   Subject: Request for Information
   Date: 2/1/2008 3:18:41 PM Eastern Standard Time
   From: janedoe@mycomputer.com
   To: webmaster@candyloversassociation.org

   I am a fifth grade student and I am interested in learning more about careers for candy lovers. Would you please send me any information you have about what people do in your industry?

   Thank you very much.
   Jane Doe

2. Write a letter requesting information.
   Your letter should be either typed on a computer or written in your best handwriting. It should include the date, the complete address of the organization you are

contacting, a salutation or greeting, a brief description your request, and a signature. Make sure to include an address where the organization can reach you with a reply. Something like the following letter would work just fine.

> Dear Sir or Madam:
>
> I am a fifth grade student and I would like to learn more about what it is like to work in the candy lover profession. Would you please send me information about careers? My address is 456 Main Street, Anytown, USA 54321
>
> Than you very much.
>
> Sincerely,
> Jane Doe

Write the names and address of the professional organizations you discover on a separate sheet of paper.

#5 CHAT ON THE PHONE

Talking to a seasoned professional—someone who experiences the job day in and day out—can be a great way to get the inside story on what a career is all about. Fortunately for you, the experts in any career field can be as close as the nearest telephone.

Sure it can be a bit scary calling up an adult whom you don't know. But, two things are in your favor:

1. They can't see you. The worst thing they can do is hang up on you, so just relax and enjoy the conversation.

2. They'll probably be happy to talk to you about their job. In fact, most people will be flattered that you've called. If you happen to contact someone who seems reluctant to talk, thank them for their time and try someone else.

Here are a few pointers to help make your telephone interview a success:

☀ Mind your manners and speak clearly.
☀ Be respectful of their time and position.
☀ Be prepared with good questions and take notes as you talk.

One more common sense reminder: Be careful about giving out your address and DO NOT arrange to meet anyone you don't know without your parents' supervision.

TRACKING DOWN CAREER EXPERTS

You might be wondering by now how to find someone to interview. Have no fear! It's easy, if you're persistent. All you have to do is ask. Ask the right people and you'll have a great lead in no time.

A few of the people to ask and sources to turn to are

Your parents. They may know someone (or know someone who knows someone) who has just the kind of job you're looking for.

Your friends and neighbors. You might be surprised to find out how many interesting jobs these people have when you start asking them what they (or their parents) do for a living.

Librarians. Since you've already figured out what kinds of companies employ people in your field of interest, the next step is to ask for information about local employers. Although it's a bit cumbersome to use, a big volume called *Contacts Influential* can provide this kind of information.

Professional associations. Call, e-mail, or write to the professional associations you discovered using the activity on pages 169–171 and ask for recommendations.

Chambers of commerce. The local chamber of commerce probably has a directory of employers, their specialties, and their phone numbers. Call the chamber, explain what you are looking for, and give them a chance to help their future workforce.

Newspaper and magazine articles. Find an article about the subject you are interested in. Chances are pretty good that it will mention the name of at least one expert in the field. The article probably won't include the person's phone number (that would be too easy), so you'll have to look for clues. Common clues include the name of the company that they work for, the town that they live in, and if the person is an author, the name of their publisher. Make a few phone calls and track them down (if long distance calls are involved, make sure to get your parents' permission first).

INQUIRING KIDS WANT TO KNOW

Before you make the call, make a list of questions to ask. You'll cover more ground if you focus on using the five W's (and the H) that you've probably heard about in your creative writing classes: Who? What? Where? When? How? and Why? For example,

1. Who do you work for?

   _____

2. What is a typical work day like for you?

   _____

3. Where can I get some on-the-job experience?

   _____

4. When did you become a _____?
   (profession)

5. How much can you earn in this profession? (But, remember it's not polite to ask someone how much *he* or *she* earns.)

   _____

6. Why did you choose this profession?

   _____

Use a grid like the one below to keep track of the questions you ask in the boxes labeled "Q," and the answers you receive in the boxes labeled "A."

Who?	What?	Where?	When?	How?	Why?
Q	Q	Q	Q	Q	Q
A	A	A	A	A	A
Q	Q	Q	Q	Q	Q
A	A	A	A	A	A

One last suggestion: Add a professional (and very classy) touch to the interview process by following up with a thank-you note to the person who took time out of a busy schedule to talk with you.

#6 INFORMATION IS POWER

As you may have noticed, a similar pattern of information was used for each of the careers profiled in this book. Each entry included:

- ☀ a general description of the career
- ☀ Try It Out activities to give readers a chance to find out what's its really like to do each job
- ☀ list of Web sites, library resources, and professional organizations to check for more information
- ☀ a get-acquainted interview with a professional

You may have also noticed that all the information you just gathered would fit rather nicely in a Career Ideas for Kids career profile of your own. Just fill in the blanks on the following pages to get your thoughts together (or, if this book does not belong to you, use a separate sheet of paper).

And, by the way, this formula is one that you can use throughout your life to help you make fully informed career choices.

CAREER TITLE _____

WHAT IS A_____?

Use career encyclopedias and other resources to write a description of this
career.

SKILL SET

✔ _____

✔ _____

✔ _____

_____

_____

_____

_____

👉 TRY IT OUT

Write project ideas here. Ask your parents and your teacher
to come up with a plan.

_____

_____

_____

_____

_____

✔ CHECK IT OUT

🖱 ON THE WEB

List Internet addresses of interesting Web sites you find.

_____

_____

_____

_____

_____

AT THE LIBRARY

List the titles and authors of books about this career.

_____

_____

_____

_____

_____

WITH THE EXPERTS

List professional organizations where you can learn more about this profession.

_____

_____

_____

_____

_____

GET ACQUAINTED

Interview a professional in the field and summarize your findings.

_____

_____

_____

_____

_____

_____

_____

WHAT'S NEXT?

Whoa, everybody! At this point, you've put in some serious miles on your career exploration journey. Before you move on, let's put things in reverse for just a sec and take another look at some of the clues you uncovered about yourself when you completed the "discover" activities in the Get in Gear chapter on pages 7 to 26.

The following activities will help lay the clues you learned about yourself alongside the clues you learned about a favorite career idea. The comparison will help you decide if that particular career idea is good idea for you to pursue. It doesn't mater if a certain career sounds absolutely amazing. If it doesn't honor your skills, your interests, and your values—it's not going to work for you.

The first time you looked at these activities they were numbered one through five as "Discover" activities. This time around they are numbered in the same order but they labeled "Rediscover" activities. That's not done to confuse you (sure hope it doesn't!). Instead, it's done to drive home a very important point that this is an important process that you'll want to revisit time and time again as you venture throughout your career—now and later.

First, pick the one career idea that you are most interested in at this point and write its name here (or if this book doesn't belong to you, blah, blah, blah—you know the drill by now):

_____

With that idea in mind, revisit your responses to the following Get in Gear activities and complete the following:

REDISCOVER #1:
WATCH FOR SIGNS ALONG THE WAY

Based on your answers to the statements on page 8, choose which of the following road signs best describes how you feel about your career idea.

- ☼ Green light—Go! Go! Go! This career idea is a perfect fit!
- ☼ Yellow light—Proceed with caution! This career idea is a good possibility but you're not quite sure that it's the "one" just yet.
- ☼ Stop—Hit the brakes! There's no doubt about—this career idea is definitely not for you!

REDISCOVER #2:
RULES OF THE ROAD

Take another look at the work-values chart you made on page 16. Now, use the same symbols to create a work-values chart for the career idea you are considering. After you have all the symbols in place, compare the two charts and answer these questions:

- ☼ Does your career idea's purpose line up with yours? Would it allow you to work in the kinds of place you most want to work in?
- ☼ What about the time commitment—is it in sync with what you're hoping for?
- ☼ Does it let you work with the tools and the kind of people you most want to work with?
- ☼ And, last but not least, are you willing to do what it takes to prepare for a career like this?

PURPOSE	PLACE	TIME

TOOLS	PEOPLE	PREPARATION

REDISCOVER #3: DANGEROUS DETOURS

Go back to page 16 and double-check your list of 10 careers that you hope to avoid at any cost.

Is this career on that list? ____Yes _____ No

Should it be? ____Yes _____ No

REDISCOVER #4:
ULTIMATE CAREER DESTINATION

Pull out the ultimate career destination brochure you made (as described on page 17). Use a pencil to cross through every reference to "my ideal career" and replace it with the name of the career idea you are now considering.

Is the brochure still true? _____Yes _____ No

If not, what would you have change on the brochure to make it true?

REDISCOVER #5:
GET SOME DIRECTION

Quick! Think fast! What is your personal Skill Set as discovered on page 26?

Write down your top three interest areas:

1. _____

2. _____

3. _____

What three interest areas are most closely associated with your career idea?

1. _____

2. _____

3. _____

Do this career's interest areas match any of yours?
_____Yes _____ No

Now the big question is this: Are you headed in the right direction?

If so, here are some suggestions to keep you moving ahead:

- Keep learning all you can about this career—read, surf the Web, talk to people, etc. In other words, keep using some of the strategies you used in the "Don't Stop Now" chapter on pages 163 to 177 to do all you can to make a fully informed career decision.
- Work hard in school and get good grades. What you do now counts! Your performance, your behavior, your attitude—all conspire to either propel you forward or hold you back.
- Get involved in clubs and other after-school activities to further develop your interests and skills. Whether it's student government, 4-H, or sports, these kinds of activities give you a chance to try new things and gain confidence in your abilities.

If not, here are some suggestions to help you regroup:

- Read other books in the Career Ideas for Kids series to explore options associated with you other interest areas.
- Take a variety of classes in school and get involved in different kids of after-school activities to get a better sense of what you like and what you do well.
- Talk to your school guidance counselor about taking a career assessment test to help fine tune your focus.
- Most of all, remember that time is on your side. Use the next few years to discover more about yourself, explore the options, and experiment with what it will take to make you succeed. Keep at it and look forward to a fantastic future!

HOORAY! YOU DID IT!

This has been quite a trip. If someone tries to tell you that this process is easy, don't believe them. Figuring out what you want to do with the rest of your life is heavy stuff, and it should be. If you don't put some thought (and some sweat and hard work) into the process, you'll get stuck with whatever comes your way.

You may not have things planned to a T. Actually, it's probably better if you don't. You'll change some of your ideas as you grow and experience new things. And, you may find an interesting detour or two along the way. That's OK.

The most important thing about beginning this process now is that you've started to dream. You've discovered that you have some unique talents and abilities to share. You've become aware of some of the ways you can use them to make a living—and, perhaps, make a difference in the world.

Whatever you do, don't lose sight of the hopes and dreams you've discovered. You've got your entire future ahead of you. Use it wisely.

PASSPORT TO YOUR FUTURE

Getting where you want to go requires patience, focus, and lots of hard work. It also hinges on making good choices. Following is a list of some surefire ways to give yourself the best shot at a bright future. Are you up to the challenge? Can you do it? Do you dare?

Put your initials next to each item that you absolutely promise to do.

___ ☼ Do my best in every class at school
___ ☼ Take advantage of every opportunity to get a wide variety of experiences through participation in sports, after-school activities, at my favorite place of worship, and in my community
___ ☼ Ask my parents, teachers, or other trusted adults for help when I need it
___ ☼ Stay away from drugs, alcohol, and other bad scenes that can rob me of a future before I even get there
___ ☼ Graduate from high school

SOME FUTURE DESTINATIONS

Wow! Look how far you've come! By now you should be well-equipped to discover, explore, and experiment your way to an absolutely fantastic future. To keep you headed in the right direction, this section will point you toward useful resources that provide more insight, information, and inspiration as you continue your quest to find the perfect career.

IT'S NOT JUST FOR NERDS

The school counselor's office is not just a place where teachers send troublemakers. One of its main purposes is to help students like you make the most of your educational opportunities. Most schools will have a number of useful resources, including career assessment tools (ask

about the Self-Directed Search Career Explorer or the COPS Interest Inventory—these are especially useful assessments for people your age). They may also have a stash of books, videos, and other helpful materials.

Make sure no one's looking and sneak into your school counseling office to get some expert advice!

AWESOME INTERNET CAREER RESOURCES

Your parents will be green with envy when they see all the career planning resources you have at your fingertips. Get ready to hear them whine, "But they didn't have all this stuff when I was a kid." Make the most of these cyberspace opportunities.

☼ **Adventures in Education**
http://adventuresineducation.org/middleschool
Here you'll find some useful tools to make the most of your education—starting now. Make sure to watch "The Great College Mystery," an online animation featuring Dr. Ed.

☼ **America's Career InfoNet**
http://www.acinet.org
Career Web sites don't get any bigger than this one! Compliments of U.S. Department of Labor, and a chunk of your parent's tax dollars, you'll find all kinds of information about what people do, how much money they make, and where they work. Although it's mostly geared toward adults, you may want to take a look at some of the videos (the site has links to more than 450!) that show people at work.

☼ **ASVAB Career Exploration Program**
http://www.asvabprogram.com
This Web site may prove especially useful as you continue to think through various options. It includes

sections for students to learn about themselves, to explore careers, and to plan for their futures.

☼ Career Voyages
http://www.careervoyages.gov
This Web site will be especially helpful to you as you get a little older. It offers four paths to get you started: "Where do I start?" "Which industries are growing?" "How do I qualify and get a job?" and "Does education pay? How do I pay?" However, it also includes a special section especially for elementary school students. Just click on the button that says "Still in elementary school?" or go to http://www.careervoyages.gov/students-elementary.cfm.

☼ Job Profiles
http://jobprofiles.org
This Web site presents the personal side of work with profiles of people working in jobs associated with agriculture and nature, arts and sports, business and communications, construction and manufacturing, education and science, government, health and social services, retail and wholesale, and other industries.

☼ Major and Careers Central
http://www.collegeboard.com/csearch/majors_careers
This Web site is hosted by the College Board (the organization responsible for a very important test called the SAT that you're likely to encounter if you plan to go to college). It includes helpful information about how different kinds of subjects you can study in college can prepare you for specific types of jobs.

☼ Mapping Your Future
http://mapping-your-future.org/MHSS/

This Web site provides strategies and resources for students as they progress through middle school and high school.

☀ My Cool Career
http://www.mycoolcareer.com
This Web site is where you can take free online self-assessment quizzes, explore your dreams, and listen to people with interesting jobs talk about their work.

☀ O*NET Online
http://online.onetcenter.org
This U.S. Department of Labor Web site provides comprehensive information about hundreds of important occupations. Although you may need to ask a parent or teacher to help you figure out how to use the system it can be a good source of digging for nitty-gritty details about a specific type of job. For instance, each profile includes a description of the skills, abilities, and special knowledge needed to perform each job.

☀ Think College Early
http://www.ed.gov/students/prep/college/
thinkcollege/early/edlite-tcehome.html
Even though you almost need a college degree just to type in the Web address for this U.S. Department of Education Web site, it contains some really cool career information and helps you think about how college might fit into your future plans.

☀ What Interests You?
http://bls.gov/k12/index
This Bureau of Labor Statistics Web site is geared towards student. It lets you explore careers by interests like reading, building and fixing things, managing money, helping people, and more.

JOIN THE CLUB

Once you've completed the eighth grade, you are eligible to check out local opportunities to participate in Learning for Life's career education programs. Some communities offer Explorer posts that sponsor activities with students interested in industries that include the arts and humanities, aviation, business, communications, engineering, fire service, health, law enforcement, law and government, science, skilled trades, or social services. To find a local officer go to http://www.learning-for-life.org/exploring/main.html and type in your zip code.

Until then, you can go online and play Life Choices, a really fun and challenging game where you get one of five virtual jobs at http://www.learning-for-life.org/games/LCSH/index.html.

MORE CAREER BOOKS ESPECIALLY FOR KIDS

It's especially important that people your age find out all they can about as many different careers as they can. Books like the ones listed below can introduce all kinds of interesting ideas that you might not encounter in your everyday life.

Greenfeld, Barbara C. and Robert A. Weinstein. *The Kids's College Almanac: A first Look at College.* Indianapolis, Ind.: JIST Works, 2001.
Young Person's Occupational Outlook Handbook. Indianapolis, Ind.: JIST Works, 2005.

Following are brief descriptions of several series of books geared especially toward kids like you. To find copies of these books ask your school or public librarian to help you search the card file or library computer system using the name of the series.

Career Connections (published by UXL)
This extensive series features information and illustrations about jobs of interest to people interested in art and design, entrepreneurship, food, government and law, history, math and computers, and the performing arts as well as for those who want to work with their hands or with living things.

Career Ideas for Kids (written by Diane Lindsey Reeves, published by Ferguson)
This series of interactive career exploration books features 10 different titles for kids who like adventure and travel, animals and nature, art, computers, math and money, music and dance, science, sports, talking, and writing.

Career Without College (published by Peterson's)
These books offer a look at options available to those who prefer to find jobs that do not require a college degree and include titles focusing on cars, computers, fashion, fitness, health care, and music.

Cool Careers (published by Rosen Publishing)
Each title in this series focuses on a cutting-edge occupation such as computer animator, hardware engineer, multimedia and new media developer, video game designer, web entrepreneur, and webmaster.

Discovering Careers for Your Future (published by Ferguson)
This series includes a wide range of titles that include those that focus on adventure, art, construction, fashion, film, history, nature, publishing, and radio and television.

Risky Business (written by Keith Elliot Greenberg, published by Blackbirch Press)
These books feature stories about people with adventurous types of jobs and include titles about a bomb squad officer, disease detective, marine biologist, photojournalist, rodeo clown, smoke jumper, storm chaser, stunt woman, test pilot, and wildlife special agent.

HEAVY-DUTY RESOURCES

Career encyclopedias provide general information about a lot of professions and can be a great place to start a career search. Those listed here are easy to use and provide useful information about nearly a zillion different jobs. Look for them in the reference section of your local library.

Career Discovery Encyclopedia, 5th Edition. New York: Ferguson Publishing, 2003

Careers for the 21st Century. Farmington Hills, Mich.: Lucent Books, 2002.

Children's Dictionary of Occupations. Princeton, N.J.: Cambridge Educational, 2004.

Encyclopedia of Career and Vocational Guidance. New York: Ferguson Publishing, 2005.

Farr, Michael and Laurence Shatkin. *Enhanced Occupational Outlook Handbook.* Indianapolis, Ind.: JIST Works, 2005.

Occupational Outlook Handbook. Washington, D.C.: U.S. Government Printing Office, 2005.

FINDING PLACES TO WORK

Even though you probably aren't quite yet in the market for a real job, you can learn a lot about the kinds of jobs you might find if you were looking by visiting some of the most popular job-hunting Web sites on the Internet. Two particularly good ones to investigate are America's Job Bank (http://www.ajb.org) and Monster (http://www.monster.com).

INDEX

Page numbers in **boldface** indicate main articles. Page numbers in *italics* indicate photographs.